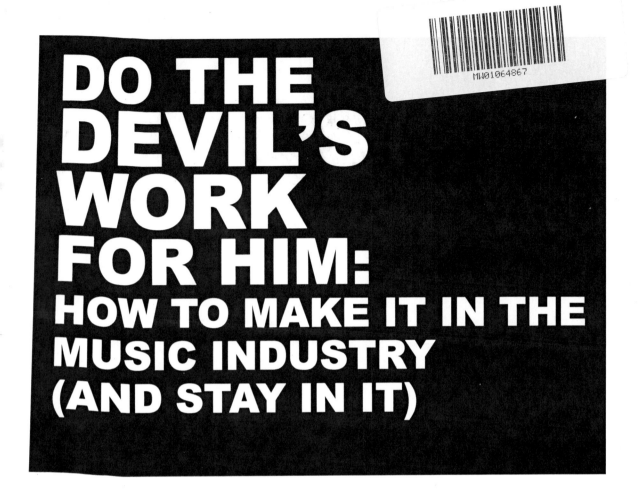

DO THE DEVIL'S WORK FOR HIM:
HOW TO MAKE IT IN THE MUSIC INDUSTRY (AND STAY IN IT)

By Amy Sciarretto & Rick Florino

McCarren Publishing

ISBN 978-0-9777863-1-2

Copyright © 2009 by Amy Sciarretto and Rick Florino

Published by McCarren Publishing with permission of the copyright holders.
Visit us on the web at www.McCarrenPublishing.com

Edited by Erin Delaney

Design & Illustration: Kevin Dougherty/Kustom Kool Media
kustomkool@gmail.com

Printed in the United States.

10 9 8 7 6 5 4 3 2 1

Everybody wants to be a rock star.

The question that we hear all the time is, "How do I get into the music industry?" Well, that's not the hard part. It's easy to get "into" the industry. The hard part is having longevity, especially when CD sales are at an all-time low, and the pie is getting smaller and smaller. However, as always, this industry is as Darwinian as the jungle. It's all about survival. We've lived it. We've survived it. And that's what we're going to teach you. The most important thing you have to remember about breaking in is: **Working in the music industry is not a job. It's a lifestyle that requires commitment.**

People will always need and love music. The business model, the playing field and the players may change, but bands are always going to need to create and fans are always going to need to see someone live and to buy music from, which requires a system and infrastructure to help sell the music to the consumer. That's where you come in.

We've come up with foolproof methods for numerous ways to make an impact behind the scenes in the industry. This vast cornucopia of options is like a giant multi-flavored vat of ice cream where you can pick the most flavorful of you and your talents.

In "DO THE DEVIL'S WORK FOR HIM: HOW TO MAKE IT IN THE MUSIC INDUSTRY (AND STAY IN IT)" we'll discuss marketing and promotions, publicity, radio DJing, video work, freelance writing, and web site building.

We'll address internships for college students and those of you who are not currently students, hopefully, you will work under a boss who teaches you what a "solid" is. (That'll come in handy later. We've got a whole chapter on it!)

You'll find that no matter where your best skills are, we'll teach you what's necessary to survive in an industry that is shrinking and getting more cutthroat and we'll show you how your love of music and our enduring music industry principles can boost you in various entertainment venues such as: companies, corporations, and industries (especially movies).

Now the fun begins, and each of us authors will provide our own perspective on each chapter's topic.— Read on and we'll show you that by the end of the day, this is rock 'n roll, and if you can't have fun while rocking and rolling, then you can't have fun anywhere, friend.

-Amy & Rick

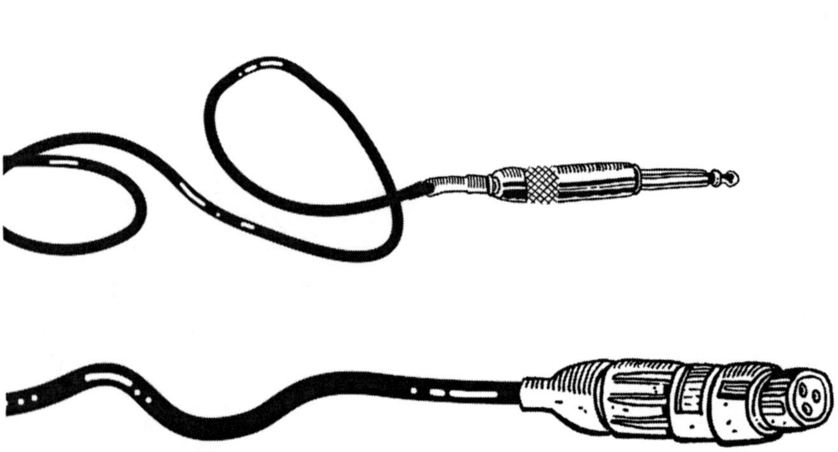

CHAPTER I

Work For Free

The best way to start off in the music industry is to work for free. Why? Let's face it: no one in their right mind is going to turn down free work. That's just reality. Free work (aka an internship) is extremely easy to obtain in the industry, especially if you're a student looking for college credit. Remember, that early bird gets the pick of those squiggly worms. And isn't working for a label for credit better than spending more time in another lecture? We'd say so.

You're getting an education in the eye of the storm, like in *Back To School* with Rodney Dangerfield. In one particular scene, Rodney Dangerfield's character, a 50-something, self-made millionaire, goes to college with his son. In Dangerfield's first business class, he shoots every theory his professor offers about business to hell and back, based on his real world, real life experience. So while theories have their place, they can't beat practical, real world, real office, in the thick-of-things experience—something all prospective employers' desire and value.

As a rule of thumb: Start early and intern at as many companies as you can. Even intern during all of your semesters. Intern for a year and then move on to another department or company. If you start in a label's publicity department, move to the promotion or A&R sector next. If you start at a label, make your next internship at a management firm. If you intern at a magazine, go to a label for the follow-up internship.

 Rick Says: The best way to start in the entertainment industry early on is to major in Communications. These include film and TV studies, filmmaking, screenwriting, music industry, journalism, so on and so forth. Most communications programs will help establish a background understanding of the industry, which is all you need. You learn the skeleton in class, and then get an internship to achieve some real life experience.

Getting an internship is pretty straightforward. This is one of the best ways to start in the entertainment industry. See if your college offers an internship program. Even if you're in school in East Nowhere, Ohio, oftentimes the school will have an affiliate program in New York or Los Angeles for students looking to break into the industry.

My first internship was at New Line Cinema in their film music department. I went to Boston University, and in the last semester of college, they offered a Los Angeles internship program based in the Park La Brea apartment community as an option for seniors in the Communications school. So basically, you can apply to this program, and if you get in you get to spend your last semester living and working in L.A. for full credit. To me, that beat the winter and being around those moronic Red Sox fans. So I followed all the steps, applied to the program, and got in.

I was lucky because I actually went to Boston University's high school, Boston University Academy, which allows juniors and seniors to start their course of study at Boston University in real college classes. By the end of high school, I had a year and a half of credits done for Boston University. So when I moved out to Los Angeles for my final semester, I was only 19, and when I returned from the internship program, I graduated Magna Cum Laude from Boston University.

Amy Says: I interned for FMQB, a local radio trade magazine, right outside of Philadelphia. I answered phones, provided radio chart statistics to label reps across all formats, hand-entered report playlists from radio stations, and wrote reviews and news for the metal section. I also made sure that one of the top editors, Mike Boyle, got a tear sheet of my reviews. He actually came to me and complimented my writing, after I had left a copy of my review in his mailbox. That subtle move earned me a compliment from a superior, and I was able to interact with the top brass in a personal way, as opposed to being the nameless intern at the copy and fax machine. I actually still do business with Mr. Boyle to this day and it was he who profiled me in a major music business trade magazine in 2007. This is a prime example of starting early and a little going a long way.

During this time, I also wrote for every magazine that would take my clips, ran my college radio station, and edited the music section of my school paper, all the while taking a full load of courses and working part time at an insurance office. Is this making you sweat? It shouldn't! Since I was interning/writing/working in a single industry by multi-tasking in several areas within a singular scene of music, it was easy to organize all my tasks.

Even if you're not in college or your college doesn't have an internship program, getting an internship is still not that hard. Thanks to that wonderful little toy known as "the Internet," it's extremely easy to get record label or magazine contact information. Just "Google" the labels that you're interested in working with. Not sure which ones those are? Just check the back of your favorite bands' CDs for the label's name. It's easy enough. Find the label's phone number or general email address and inquire about "possible internship" opportunities. Send them a short introduction: just one or two sentences about who you are and that you're looking for an internship.

Now, it's hard to turn down free work, but sometimes labels do, especially if you're not in college or they don't need anyone at the time. Still, it's not impossible to get the position; be persistent and hit up every label, film studio, magazine or management firm, or radio station that you can. If you have a friend who DJs at a radio station, then ask him if he has a contact at the label you are interested in interning for, and ask for some info. Use every little resource, no matter how small or big it is. Show the label initiative and ingenuity. Every employer wants to hire a go-getter.

Here's an example on how to establish contact:

> Introductory Email Example:
> Hello,
> My name is _____, and I'm a senior at _____.
> I'm contacting you regarding possible internship opportunities at your company. I have attached my resume and cover letter, but would also like to know who I can forward this to in your Human Resources department. I look forward to your response.
> Sincerely,
>
> _____

Keep it short, sweet, and simple. That's the best way to get the attention of that HR contact at the company where you're interested in working. Always attach your resume and cover letter, because it gives the respondent less to do. They'll already have your information on file, and don't have to exchange dozens of emails with you. Clogging their inbox is *not* the way to go. There's no need to burden them in the introductory email with all of those cool summer jobs on your resume, so save it for the interview.

Also, if you've made contacts at the label through any other means, use that contact. It's best to have a direct person who can forward your contact along, as opposed to a blind cold query, which can linger in an inbox for days, weeks, or months before it's deleted without even being read. If someone you know passes along your info, it's almost like an inherent recommendation from them. Someone isn't going to pass along your info if they don't have a good opinion of you. Why? Because it makes them look bad. But if you don't have these inside, in-house contacts already through any side work you may do, then utilize those extra services at your college if they're available to you.

Getting an internship through your college and its career planning center is the easiest way to start. Colleges will often put you up in housing, and they have contacts that you can reach out to in order to find an internship. They also have alumni relations and there may be a contact that was just like you, only five years ago.Most importantly, always use a "professional" email address.You don't need your email address to be through your lawyer's firm or anything like that, but don't email the HR person at your prospective internship from **BloodDrinker666@xyzmail.com** either. Instead opt for the standard **yourname@gmail.com** or even your college email address, such as joe_student@college.edu. It's free, holds a ton of emails, and it sounds more professional than **im_a_psycho_you_shouldnt_hire@zzz.com**.

 Rick Says: So I moved out to LA from Boston, and BU had it all setup. They had housing in a fantastic area of LA inside Park LaBrea, and they offered their three required classes right in one of the apartments at Park LaBrea. The fourth source of credit was the internship, and I contacted about twenty studios and production companies (When you're new in the industry, you have to be persistent and willing to work for your internship.) Granted, once people meet you, it's hard for them to turn down free work, but you have to be compelling enough for them to set up that initial interview. Once I got the internship, the school aided in my success by providing a directory of every studio with a contact for the internship coordinator..

The best way to get that interview is to write a great cover letter and resume. Contact your college's HR department or look online for templates, and you'll easily be able to come up with something hot. Once you do get your interview, dress up. We're not talking black tie; we're talking dress pants, a dress shirt, and a tie. Or a suit. Ladies, a dress or skirt are appropriate, but don't be afraid to showcase your personal style, as well. You've got to dress for the job you want, not the one you've got. So don't look like you're going to interview for that "amazing," summer security gig at Target. You're trying to break into an industry where image does play a part. It's not everything, but be professional.

Rick Says: I remember I wore a suit to my New Line interview. Everyone in New Line's music department was clad in jeans and t-shirts, but the truth is, you can never be overdressed. Granted, the opportunity for you to express yourself through personal style is not a license to wear a *My Cousin Vinny*-style purple tuxedo. Instead try and look like George Clooney or Brad Pitt in *Ocean's 11*. I'd like to think I did anyway.

Amy Says: Ladies, when I interviewed at CMJ New Music Report, Concrete Marketing, and TVT Records right out of college, it was May in NYC, and it was warm, so I wore cute knee-length dresses and platform Mary Janes. It was professional, but showed my funky style, and proved that I would fit into the rock 'n' roll environments that I was trying to break into. It's great to wear earrings and jewelry, but keep it to a minimum and keep it to your style. You are looking to break into this industry, and you want to accurately represent yourself. Just do it in your Sunday best. No hoochie outfits, no busting out all over, and no hanging out in all the wrong places. You want to leave an impression, albeit a good one. Most importantly, be comfortable. Wear something that makes you feel confident. And don't do anything major, like cut or change the color of your hair the day before the interview. You want to be confident and comfortable in your own skin, and put forth the best possible you.

As an extension of my wardrobe, I always carried a bound portfolio of the reviews I had amassed during my college years (I started out writing for *Chord* for free CDs and tickets, which snowballed into writing for *Juice* for free CDs, tickets, *and payment* for each assignment) so that I could hand them to my interviewer before he or she asked, which made me appear professional as well as prepared for the job.

Once you do get your internship, bust your ass! The work is not going to be that interesting or glamorous, so accept this unassailable fact before walking in the door. This is your first shot at being in the industry. Every copy that you make for someone must be perfect. Make coffee to the exact specifications that you're given. Deliver packages around the office quickly. Most importantly, have a HUGE smile on your face the whole time. Talk to everyone that you can. If you're at a magazine, fact check a music review like it's a classified document for the Pentagon. If you hate the music you've been assigned to review, do it with a smile and don't let on that you're not into it…until you've established yourself and have built a rapport within your environment.

Rick Says: At New Line, I made friends with everyone from the music executives to the janitors, because I was always happy while I was there. The company will be way more likely to keep you around if you're happy and bringing in good energy. Granted, it sounds hippie-ish, but it's true. People love a happy dude in the office. Even if the work is boring, it's better than security at Target, even with the great discount, right?

Amy Says: When I was at FMQB, I dropped out of a Master's level Literary Theory and Criticism class and had to take an 'incomplete' for it, but I made sure that I stayed as late as my boss, asked him what else I could do for him, asked for more work, and never said I was too busy to help the rock radio department update their databases and files. When I answered the phones and gave out chart stats to promo execs I had never met, I made sure to ask their name, and then I called them by it. For example, if a call came in from Jen at Roadrunner, I would say, "Hi Jen! It's Amy, Bram's assistant. He's on a call, but I'll make sure to get him on with you right away." I made sure that the people calling my boss knew I was there if they needed anything. 9 times out of 10, the caller would say, "Oh, if he's on a call, can you just grab me the chart position and spin count on my band quickly?" The caller ended up happy and got what they wanted without having to wait.

We know that working for free sucks. What sucks even more is doing boring work for free. However, we all had to do it, so get over it. Work for free now, so you can collect a check later because as Gina Gershon's character laments in *Showgirls:* "There's always someone younger and hungrier coming up the stairs behind you." If you don't do it, there's someone else who will. So, own your opportunities. No task is too small for you to do. If you can't manage the most mundane of tasks, no one is going to trust you with something larger and more important.

Rick Says: I did some pretty mundane and lame work at New Line during my internship. I had to manually burn hundreds of CDs, make coffee for people and copy hundreds of thousands of script pages. The most interesting thing I got to do was answer the phone for a week while one of the department's assistants was gone, but it was awesome. I'd filter calls coming through from the offices of everyone from *Rush Hour* and *Red Dragon* director Brett Ratner to Wu Tang Clan's RZA. But that was the beginning. They didn't let all of the interns answer the phones, but they knew that they could trust me because I'd worked to become a reliable asset.

My New Line internship boss, James Patrick, became one of my best friends in Los Angeles, and he even helped me get two jobs. In fact, both of my first "real world" gigs were a byproduct of that New Line internship. One of the music executives at New Line got me a job as his wife's assistant at an independent electronica label. Granted, the genre wasn't really my thing, but all entry-level jobs are the same, it doesn't matter where you are. I also got a job in the New Line mailroom, because everyone liked me while I interned.

Internships are how you make contacts. So make friends at your internship, work extremely hard, be charismatic, and always be upbeat, people will remember you. Say hello to everyone and get to know their names. No matter what is going on in your life at the time, the second you enter that office during the day, act like you are at Disneyland. That's how you make and keep contacts. You need those contacts early on, because this business is all about relationships and how well you begin, maintain, and develop them. The more people that you have on your side, the better.

 Amy Says: At FMQB, owner Kal Rudman had me photocopy drawings that local kindergartners had made for him. Sure, I would have preferred to answer phones for my boss and give out chart stats, but what was a few minutes making copies for the guy who runs the joint?

Be early to your internship and stay late. Granted the work is mundane but you're still an "intern." Treat your internship like a full-time job while developng your business etiquette and making friendships with everyone you can. It's a rite of passage that we all go through so make the most of it.

 Amy Says: I have managed about thirty interns over the course of my career. Many of them were stellar. Several were complete bombs who were excellent in their interviews with me and in their work ethic and quality, but once on the floor in the environment, they cracked, or showed they didn't have the common sense or basic office decorum. Remember: even though this is a cool industry that is fun and can be a dream-come-true, it's also a business. Conduct yourself as though you are working at a *Fortune 500* Company or a bank. Be polite. Be respectful. Express yourself, but don't offend people. Don't listen in on people's conversations or interrupt them. I know this should seem like something I don't have to tell you, but I thought this many times with interns who should have known it to be common sense, but I was wrong and I was embarrassed by their actions. You never ever want to make your boss look bad, so keep in mind that you, as an intern, should be seen and not heard. If people see you hustling and bustling, then they will allow you to be heard. Yes, it seems like you're a serf toiling away here, but remember: You're starting at the bottom and if you adhere to these rules, you'll move up quickly.

Now there are a few other ways to break into the industry when you don't know anyone. If you want magazine experience, then ask the editor if you can distribute copies somewhere or deliver them to their contacts as a gopher. Join a street team or e-team for your favorite band either through the label or a promotional company. These teams will take pretty much anyone, and they allow you to help promote the band. In exchange, they'll often hook you up with meet and greets and concert tickets. This isn't as good of a way to break in as getting an internship, but it'll do. If you really work hard on the street team, your work ethic will show through, and will separate you from your peers.

Rick Says: When I started out, I did street team work for Black Label Society. I got about 800 samplers for the *1919 Eternal* record, dropped them off at record stores, and handed them out at every show I went to. However, street teaming is not as important as getting involved in the e-teams. You'll post bulletins on MySpace and send out various e-blasts to spread the word. Doing that work is just a great resume item, and it does get you a few contacts and a foot in the door. You're not going to get paid, but if you're helping your favorite band, just enjoy it. There's a good chance you'll even get to meet them as a byproduct of being on the team.

 Amy Says: I was a "Foot Soldier" for Victory Records' street team in 1997. At the time, street teams were just taking off, I adored the label and 95% of its roster, and I had already known Ron, their radio rep, from running my college station. But this street team gig opened up access to the retail department and the press department after I checked retail stock, dropped off flyers and promo in-store play copies at local Philadelphia record stores, hung posters at venues and lifestyle shops like tattoo parlors, and put stickers on drive-thru menus and stop signs. I was also able to make contacts in deeper parts of the company, thus opening up the possibilities for future employment. Because I was such a dedicated supporter of the label, I was offered a job twice, but didn't want to move to Chicago and instead chose local, East Coast gigs. Looking back, the gig was much more guerilla than current street teams, which are now more online-oriented, but it was fun to carry a knapsack full of promo material from bands I loved and have kids at shows come up to me asking for promo material because they thought I worked for Victory. I went from having to fight other fans at shows for the promo posters on the walls of the venue to having a few copies signed and framed on the wall of my bedroom (Isn't the love of the music why you are trying to break into this crazy business in the first place?) So take note: if you are an exemplary teamer, you will have access to cool perks like autographed and rare merch.

Another way to break into the industry is to write. If you can write well and you want to write, this is the most fulfilling break-in strategy (and our personal favorite). Start by writing for yourself. Review every CD that you get and every concert that you attend. Share the reviews with your friends and see what they think. And most importantly, we cannot stress the importance of reading; it's the best way to become inspired to write. So, read everything and read often!

 Rick Says: Pick some favorite writers and follow their styles to see what makes them distinct, then create your own. Some of my favorite music writers are Paul Gargano, David Fricke, and my writing partner, Amy Sciarretto. They've all influenced me in some way, but over the years, I've crafted my own style. I had a little notebook that I carried everywhere, and wrote numerous concert reviews. I thought after I finished at New Line, I was going to become a rock star. That didn't happen, so while I was working at that electronica label, my mom suggested I write about music. It made sense.

In the notebook, which ironically my mom bought me from Target right before I moved to Los Angeles, I started reviewing every single show I went to and every CD that I got. One day, my old internship boss at New Line saw the notebook and checked out my review of Slipknot at the Forum. He was kind enough to give it to Paul Gargano, who was Editor-in-Chief of *Metal Edge* at the time, and he was into my writing and became my mentor. See, that internship at New Line really started it all for me!

I knew it was important that I maintained contact with my boss there, so after doing some stuff for *Metal Edge*, I built up a portfolio, and I started hitting up every magazine possible (You need to prove yourself in this game.). I wrote for free at *AMP*, *Lollipop*, and *Thrasher* too, because most lower-level publications don't pay. I freelanced like that for a whole year, doing as many assignments as I could get. I probably completed 100 interviews that year, and I didn't see one dime from any of it. It didn't matter though, because I got my first two cover stories, made a ton of contacts with labels and publicity companies, and got to talk to a lot of great bands in the process.

One of my best habits since I started writing has been making sure I immediately sent my pieces to the respective publicists that coordinated the stories, even before they would run. I still do. I'd tell them to feel free to quote it, because that would increase my profile, and I'd get their feedback. That builds trust and when you hook publicists up, in return, they're more likely to hook you up. Off the bat, you're not going to get to talk to Slipknot at Baskin Robbins for that brilliant "Heavy Metal on Ice" story—pitting metal's masked marauders against 31 flavors. But, once a publicist trusts you and knows that you'll come through, you'll eventually get those cool stories.

 Amy Says: Writing for free was the foundation on which I built my writing empire. I've been writing and have been published since early 1994. I started out writing for free CDs. I edited the music section of my college paper, and since no one would submit articles and the staff was small, I had to fill pages, so I wrote about what I loved and built clips and learned to write about other music.

My first published review was Texas Is The Reason! That was good enough for me. I didn't have to buy 'em, and I still got 'em. That snowballed into being able to go to the shows for free and interview bands that I loved in person at the venue before the show. That was payment enough for me.

Because I had been bitten by the writing bug, I would send all of my clips to local magazines and ask if I could write. Because I had a bounty of clips that proved I was published, the gigs came flowing in. The clincher? I started getting paid. It may have been $5 a review, but it was still payment for my work. Then, I started to receive payment from *Juice*, a skate/surf/rock rag as well as *Chord*, a music mag in Philly that I still write for to this day. I also wrote two to three metal reviews a week for FMQB while I interned, so by the time I graduated, I had a body of nationally published work, relationships with publicists, and a well-known, well-published byline. So when I was looking for an in-house writing job at a magazine as well as publicity gigs at record labels, I was able to get clever and send out a press release on my graduation and availability for work (written in the style of the opening monologue of *The Real World)* as well as a press kit on myself, with my best clips, showing I had relationships with major magazines. I also used an Op-Ed piece that was written about me in the college newspaper and sent that with my resume. I learned early that no one could be a better publicist for Amy Sciarretto than Amy Sciarretto herself.

From this, I got the job at *CMJ New Music Report* as the editorial assistant. I was the lead candidate for gigs at TVT, Victory and Concrete Marketing, but I wanted the CMJ gig, because I remembered that I used to sit in WCCR, my college radio station, and read the Loud Rock section wishing that I was the writer. I made that dream come true.

When I started at *CMJ,* I basically wrote one review per weekly issue, re-wrote news press releases into news items, and coded, cut, and pasted content for the website. Within three months, I was promoted to *Loud Rock Editor*, with my own column. Eventually, I was known as "CMJAmy" and I expanded the section from one page of editorial and one chart to five pages of editorial and two charts, the second of which I spent a year researching and developing while establishing relationships with major market commercial radio programmers, and as a result, it became the mag's most popular column.

I parlayed this into writing gigs for the international music/hard rock Bible known as *Kerrang, Guitar World, Metal Maniacs, Revolver*, where I created two news columns. At *Revolver*, I was even lauded by the Editor-In-Chief in an interview that he did for a magazine as "knowing her shit and making us look like we know our shit." I also have written for *Hit Parader, Decibel, Alternative Press, Kerrang*, the defunct *Rockpile, Guitar World, VH1.com, Teen People, spin.com, music.com, AMP, CMJ Monthly, Mean Street, Smug, Hails & Horns, Outburn, The Aquarian Weekly*, and even helped start *Ruin*—Rick's magazine. I also hosted two shows on Sirius Satellite Radio's Hard Attack Channel for two years because I was the girl who knew the most about metal. I wrote bios for major and indie labels, for platinum selling and baby (or new) bands. *Rebel Ink* and *Urban Ink* have came knocking on my door, as well.
So from writing small reviews for free, I became an international writer just by taking on more assignments, getting my name out there, and developing a respected byline. You name the mag, and I can tell you I've probably written for it.

Nowadays, I don't have to pitch myself or provide samples to music mags because my byline is well-known. Some mags I am still with; others I eventually moved on from, but I cherish the experiences and the ink. Some mags give me assignments on what they want me to cover; others, like *Hit Parader*, give me cart blanche where I can cover whatever I want, whenever I want. But after developing my name and my reputation as a tastemaker, that's when the label gigs game calling.
You build a house brick by brick, my friends. Brick by brick. So don't expect to write me an email and ask me to help you write for a major national publication if you haven't done the things laid out in this book.

Rick Says: After you've got one internship, get another one. Internships aren't that hard to get once you have one. Plus, you can already add your internship to your current resume. The second internship that I got was directly because I worked at New Line. One of the music executives at New Line took such a liking to me that he recommended me as an intern for an electronica label that his wife worked for. I split my time wisely. I worked at New Line two days a week and at the electronica label two days a week. So I was able to have two great resume builders and experience working at a film studio and a record label. Plus, I even got paid by the label. After I applied for numerous studio jobs and got turned down, I landed my first "industry" gig as an assistant at the electronica label. So, each and every contact comes in handy. You see the same people in this game, the whole time. No one goes anywhere. It's just like the mob, once you're made, you're made. However, it's not easy to get to that point. So definitely diversify. If you have the time, intern for three companies! It's only going to make you that much stronger of a candidate for a real job once you're ready, plus, look at it this way, you get triple the contacts, and none of the work is that hard.

IN SUMMATION: Start early and start young. Intern at one company for a year. Then move onto another company and/or department to DIVERSIFY. The more diverse you are, the more marketable you become. Work a lot and work for free, and never ever leave before your boss.

BOTTOM LINE:

Work for free
Get an internship
Make contacts
Join a street team
Write for yourself

CHAPTER II

Hit The Internet Hard

So you want to write about music or movies, but *RollingStone* and *Variety* don't return your calls for some reason. That reason is probably because you're brand new to the game.

Amy Says: I get asked all the time, "Amy, how did you get your start?" and "I want to write for *Revolver* or *Decibel* like you did, so how do I get in there?" I know this might sound cocky, but I would reply as such, since it's the truth: "Major, national, glossy print mags don't take unknown writers, and if you are just starting out, you're certainly not at my level." I'm not trying to be a dick here, but it's the truth. You have to have a byline that is known, respected, and heavily published. But this begs this question: How do you get a byline that is known, respected, and initially published? That's what we are here to tell you how to do. Start early. Write a lot. Write for free. The Internet is your new BFF, so snuggle up accordingly.

Rick Says: I sent query emails and letters to over 100 publications initially, worldwide, and every one of them either didn't respond or turned me down. So, I did the next best thing. I started my very own web site. Now, I didn't know anything about starting web sites. All I knew how to do was open Internet Explorer and check my MySpace page. However, I knew that I'd need a place to write if I were ever going to be able to garner any sort of attention. So, I started my very own web site and called it "Metal N More" (www.metalnmore.com). The site looked horrible initially, but I didn't care. I was so excited. I just bought the domain name on a whim one Saturday in June of 2005, then I got this easy-to-use online web page development program, and I made a simple five page web site. It featured all of my CD reviews, show reviews, and some links to sites that I liked. It wasn't *MTV. com*, but it was something. Most of the time "something" is all it takes. That week, I managed to even convince Relapse Records and Metal Blade to send me free CDs to review. I was so nervous to cold call the labels, but once I struck up conversations with their respective publicists, it was a breeze. I was stoked to get those first free CDs. Now I can't find a place to put all of these CDs that I get every week.

I even conducted my very first interviews for Metal N More. It was a logical step from writing CD and show reviews. I just needed to convince someone to give me an interview. It's best to go with who you know, and I had one promoter friend that was able to hook up an in person interview with Matt Mc-Donough, Mudvayne's drummer. That was the beginning of a very long and industrious interview career. Of course, I featured that on Metal N More, and once I had that, I was able to send it around to all of the other publicists and show them what Metal N More was doing, and that we had interview capability, and it soared from there. After the first month, I had five interviews on there and even started getting photo passes and free tickets to shows. Again, it's all about relationships. Publicists liked me, because I was very appreciative, I could write well, and I hooked them up. If you hook people up, they will hook you up. Don't complain that you didn't get to talk to the singer or that your photo pass was only good for the support acts, appreciate every little thing early on, and it'll go even further.

Amy Says: When I first started as *CMJ*'s **Loud Rock Editor** in January 1999, I did a review of Staind's album, *Dysfunction*. It was the first piece of positive national press the then up-and-coming band received. Their publicist Anne Kristoff was so thrilled about the article, because this was a baby band that needed love early on, that she never forgot it. So even when Pantera toured with Black Sabbath off-cycle, which means the label wasn't promoting a new album, and therefore didn't have a lavish ticket budget, Anne always went out of her way to get me tickets to these shows. I remember flipping open the Columbia House catalogue and seeing my Staind review quoted there. Elektra got tons of mileage out of that quote, and a little went a long way. I cemented my relationship with the publicist and the label, and while I was writing for many national mags at the time, I always felt I was a priority for her when I needed Phil Anselmo for an interview.

Rick Says: Be sure to send every link that you make to an article to the publicist. Don't be shy either; feel free to ask them to post that on the band's MySpace or web site. If it's positive press, it only helps everyone, and then it increases your site's visibility in the eyes of other publicists and record labels. Make no mistake, either. Bands love seeing you gush about their music, so they are more than thrilled to post YOUR words on THEIR site. That's the whole point of press: spreading the word. The exchanging of links or URLs is easy and free, and benefits all parties involved.

Since you're a nobody (for now) starting a web site, you need as much of a boost as you can get! Also, take EVERY interview they offer. If you interview their brand new baby bands, they'll be more likely to hook you up with the big ones later on.

Amy Says: Since I gave Staind love early on when no one knew who they were, when they were selling millions of records I was always given first dibs on interviewing them when they were in demand. When I wanted to cover an intimate AC/DC gathering at the Hard Rock Café (where vocalist Brian Johnson promptly kissed me on the forehead when I was introduced to him), Anne made sure I got access and time with the legends. If you give some space and ink to up and coming bands now, it will benefit you later. It will also cement your relationship with bands and your reputation as a tastemaker. One of the most rewarding perks of this job is to say "I was there when they were starting out." When Kittie was preparing for the release of their Gold-selling debut, *Spit*, I was the first American writer to give them national press, and I was awarded a Gold plaque by their label, who always remembered that I devoted column inches to the band. Same thing with Slipknot and A Perfect Circle. I have Gold plaques hanging on my walls at home, as I was awarded these from labels for my dedication to helping them break their bands. While it's of course an exuberant ego massage to receive these accolades, what's more important is that giving bands ink first creates your role and reputation as a tastemaker. When you have this reputation, labels want music in your hands and in your ears first, because you will be essential in creating the buzz they need to break a band. With magazines croaking left and right, the Internet and your website will be essential in filling this role. However, again it's all about rites of passage.

Rick Says: You have to bust your ass. It's about proving yourself. We've all been there, and we've all worked for it. The music industry isn't for everyone, but if you want to be a part of it, you can. Initially, I started interviewing over seven bands a week, just to get that experience. The more musicians you talk to, the better you'll get, and the more your name will spread. You're not making any money from your web site at this point, so it's time to just build your name, repertoire, and credits.

The only way to get better at writing is to write, so if you can do a 200-word review on a new band that a publicist is pushing, what's the harm? Review and write about everything you get early on. Publish as much as you can on your web site and use your name on everything. Create your own bylines and that will increase search-ability. It sounds crazy, but where you show up on Google when people search for your name is very important these days.

After you've got your site up and running, make the rounds. Find other metal web sites and offer to write for them in exchange for links. You want your name all over the place. When publicists see your name, they'll be more likely to give you those cool interviews.

In summary, when you build your web site, make a professional, easy-to-use web site to showcase your work and resume. Send the links to the label, publicist, and promoter. Do the work FOR them. If you tell them, "hey, go check out my site," they are less apt to do it. So give them a cut and paste clip that'll make them WANT to explore your site further.

 Rick Says: That web site will serve as the building block toward something much bigger. My site, Metal N More, even eventually evolved into a full color, glossy metal magazine that landed in every Hot Topic in the United States. That took only a year. Amy and I had become friends by then, but since my name was popping up everywhere on the net, and I'd gotten my first few bylines in glossy national publications, it all began working out. I did my first BIG interviews for that site. I got to talk to Mudvayne, Shadows Fall, Strapping Young Lad, Disturbed, Mastodon and many more, all for that simple site that I built on a whim. That was only in the first six months of having it. Once I developed contacts with the amazing Mitch Schneider Organization (MSO PR), I cemented relationships and more importantly friendships that will last forever. MSO hooked me up with OZZfest photo passes, KoRn photo passes and many more, because I reviewed every release they had for Metal N More, and I took every interview opportunity that they had. I also made sure to immediately send links to my pieces, and of course, I always thanked the publicist. Courtesy goes a long way in this industry.

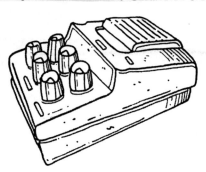

IN SUMMATION: Build a web site. Make a professional, easy-to-use website to showcase your work and resume. Send the links to the label, publicist, and promoter. Do the work FOR them.

BOTTOM LINE:

Publish your own content

Cover anything and everything that you're offered

Send the publicists, promoters and managers the exact links to their band's coverage

Put your name on everything to increase personal SEO and searchability
In the Internet age, this is a stepping stone to writing for magazines

Contacts, Contacts, Contacts!

CHAPTER III

We're not talking about the disc-shaped lenses that make you see better, we're talking about rubbing elbows. This business is all about who you know, and that's followed by what you know. Your contacts are your lifeblood, your key to success, and without them, you cannot unlock any of the doors to your career and your future.

When you meet a new contact, exchange business cards. Follow up the next day with a quick, "hey, it was great to meet you last night" email. Put them in your rolodex. Put them in your Outlook contacts. Be in their faces, so they remember you. But don't be annoying. There is a fine line between persistence and annoyance, and you need to toe that line with absolute care.

Rick Says: Even in the age of PDAs, Treos, iPhones, Blackberrys, and Sidekicks, get some business cards made. I know it's awesome that you can program everyone that you meet into your phone, but have something tangible that represents you to exchange with people. Don't be a hippie! You don't need to worry about wasting paper to make business cards. There are enough trees. Print out some business cards ASAP. You need them. It's important. If you don't believe us, watch that scene in *American Psycho* again, those cards mean a lot. Professional, glossy business cards are cheap and easy to make through great online sites like VistaPrint.com. Keep the card simple. All you need is your name, one phone number, one email address, and a web site if you've got one. Also throw in your title: writer, record producer, janitor, carpet cleaner, whatever it is you aspire to do and have begun to do for free. I printed up about a thousand business cards for Metal N More, and I gave them out to everyone that I met. Not only did it spread my name, but it branded the web site, and gave the impression of professionalism. Once publicists, managers, and promoters saw the image of professionalism, then checked our site and realized that I could write, they always hooked me up. One good friend from Century Media, publicist extraordinaire George Vallee, even got me a few gigs writing for *Thrasher Magazine*. I had done numerous interviews with God Forbid, Manntis and Behemoth for him on the site and a few other local magazines. He needed someone to write a piece for Thrasher, and he knew that I could write, and he could trust me with his contacts. I nailed it on the piece, and it ran shortly after. I couldn't believe it when I saw my piece in every 7/11 and book store that I went to. That happened less than a year after I started my web site. It doesn't take very long. Once you build relationships with publicists and record labels and maintain them, that's key to success. Everyone wants to work with someone they can trust with their contacts. So if you're referred for a gig, nail it. Prep for it as much as you can, and then knock it out of the park. You want each gig to reflect positively on you. If your friend is happy, he or she will find more cool gigs for you, and you'll possibly gain a new friend.

Amy Says: I couldn't agree more. Make your own business cards, and hand them out to people. Join professional networks like *Linked In* or *The Biz*, and reach out to connect to publicists and label personnel that way. Even though I have been writing professionally for half my life and most labels know my name and my byline, I still carry business cards in my handbag because you never know *who* you are going to meet and at any opportune time.

That's what it's about: building a business/social network. Don't be afraid to ask the publicists to hang out or get dinner. Nine times out of ten, they will also be inviting you out for drinks or to meet up before a show. What's more is that in the day and age where advance CDs are going the way of the pterodactyl, publicists will invite you to their office to listen to new music to review. Whenever you can, take them up on those offers. Because it gives you face time with them.

We're all on the same team at the end of the day. We're all music fans, and we're all promoting good music. This is rock 'n' roll, people. We should all be conducting our business with smiles on our faces. If you can't have fun in this job, and befriend those who you conduct business relations with, then you definitely are in the wrong field. We've become friends with most of the publicists that we've worked with, and it's key to doing business. It's a small microcosm. We're all fans in this business. That's why you started interning in music: because you love it. You have to love this, because it's a long hard road, as we've mentioned before, and will continue to mention ad nauseam.

When you request an interview or a CD from a publicist, always ask them what else they're working. We know you want to talk to Slipknot; everyone else does too. We've interviewed them more times than we can count. They rule. However, try and hook the publicist up a little bit too. Work with the baby bands, because those are often a priority. The label knows you want Slipknot, but give the label something to make it worth their while. Cover every lower level band, just to get that KoRn interview. It's worth it at the end of the day.

Amy Says: This is what's called "doing a solid." We devote a whole chapter to the "solid" later, but it's worth mentioning early and often. If you do a publicist or a label "a solid" by giving ink or column inches to their up 'n coming band in desperate need of press, they will remember that when you submit your request for that hard-to-nail-down platinum selling band. If the publicist knows that they can count on you, they will return the favor. It's basic business relationship maintenance and nurturing 101. Whether you're selling CDs or fine wines or widgets.

Rick Says: I was friendly and nice to everyone that I met and now I have 600 contacts in my Sidekick, with about 1000 in my Outlook. My very good friend, Gary Richards, once told me, "You see the same people on the way down that you do on the way up in the music industry." There's nothing more true. Everyone that you meet will come back—from the street teamers to the publicists. Even though one publicist may be working all lower level bands right now, she could end up handling Slayer the next record cycle, so try and work together with everyone that approaches you. Things are so shaky and fickle that everyone will move around numerous times, and that's cool, but keep your friends close!

Amy Says: I still talk to some radio contacts that I made in 1995. You never know where people are going to end up, and whose help you may need down the road. So always hold onto your contacts. If you don't, that's career suicide before it's even born. Even if your old friend who programmed a radio station in Northern Michigan is now working for a pharmaceutical company, there is no harm in staying in touch. He may eventually wind up having a career overhaul and working for a major industry firm, or he may be just able to help you get cheap medicine if you get sick!

 Rick Says: Feel free to make MySpace or Facebook friends with your contacts as well. It shows personality and adds a human element to your relationship. Often, we build up highly "textual" email and IM relationships with people in this business, but if a publicist goes out of his or her way to get you those front row Linkin Park tickets for the show you want to review, call and thank them. It goes a long way. Of course, again, have that review up the next morning with the link emailed right to the publicist. However, try to meet up with the label and publicity people at the shows. Get to know everyone that you can, because you want to increase your access more than anything else. Each person can affect that, especially if everyone likes you.

 Amy Says: Also remember that taking care of writers is the publicist's job. But don't ask for things out of range. If you don't write about crooners, then you shouldn't be asking the publicist if they can score you Neil Diamond tickets just because your mom is a fan. The publicist is doing a job and so are you, so don't abuse it. Believe us, publicists do communicate with each other, and you don't want to develop a reputation for being a "user" and "abuser" of the perks. Nowadays, labels are cutting expenses and budgets, and ticket budgets are nowhere near the size they used to be, so if a publicist tells you that he or she can only provide a single ticket in the major market show you are attending, accept it. There is no need for a label to provide a ticket so your buddy can get in for free too; your pal didn't do anything to promote the artist, but you did, so you get the perk. Don't get greedy. Remember: anything extra is always nice but not always deserved.

Nurturing your contacts is super-crucial to your success and building up a formidable network that you can grow and evolve with. So be sure to keep contact with everyone. Anytime you get a business card, email that person the next day. Always follow-up. Be in their faces, but not annoying.

In Summation: Keep in touch with all your contacts. Do the work for them and try and get that face time. Make friends with these people and help them out as much as possible. Even if they're working Skrape now, they might get Down the next album. So be nice!

BOTTOM LINE:

Cherish and nurture your contacts!

Get Used to NO... Accept it, But Don't Settle

CHAPTER IV

Now that you've got the basics on how to make contacts and where to start digging to build your music business empire, we're here to shed a little reality on the situation. Just because you think you're good enough to write for major, glossy, national mags, that's your own perception and not reality. You aren't going to send clips and a query letter to the editor-in-chief of one of these mags and get a response, begging for your services. You need them, not the other way around by any stretch.

So, after you've assembled a decent amount of clips and a press kit on yourself and your work, hit up your local entertainment and arts weeklies. Since you're a local, those magazines are more apt to take you on as a writer. Become a local scenester/beat writer that way. Reach out to the managing editor of every one of those weeklies or dailies, and send them clips. Don't ask them if they'd like to see clips; SEND THEM ANYWAY. DO THE WORK FOR THEM! Forget the "references available on request" tagline. Give it to them before they have the chance to ask.

Take initiative. Chances are, the labels and publicists are too busy dealing with too many writers and too many bands to respond back asking for clips or to look them up themselves. Do more than send a link for them to click on; the click-thru rate will be low. Send the link *and* cut and paste the text you'd like them to view. Getting it done in one fell swoop is much better than making them do one more step. Marketing studies conducted on online promotions prove this fact; the more you make someone click to another page or screen, the less they want to do it, no matter what the incentive.

Next, go to your local music store or bookstore and pick three to five magazines you'd like to write for. Buy them and familiarize yourself with their content if you no longer or don't currently read these publications. Know what they cover, so you can be well-informed about their product when you pitch your services to them. You want to help enhance their product, and you can do it with confidence. Just be smart about it.

When constructing a query to a magazine, don't consult a guidebook (other than this one, of course!) and send a generic cover letter to the magazine's editor introducing yourself in three paragraphs. Borrrr-rrrring. Chances are, they have 25 copies of those cluttering their desks or their floor anyway. Also, a lot of these editors have been in their positions for 20-30 years, so they are crusty, jaded, cynical, and have lost their passion, so it's your job to show them yours and maybe, just maybe, reawaken theirs. Okay, the latter is an extreme long shot, but the former is true. Plenty of times, a publicist will pitch a story to a magazine, and if the magazine bites but doesn't have a writer solidified or chosen for the piece, the publicist will pitch a writer, saying, "So-and-so is so into the band and will be able to ask provocative questions." When the publicist is that close to closing the deal and securing the feature, he or she will recommend a writer to get the piece one step closer to being nailed down, and thus, doing the work FOR the editor, saving the editor time tracking down a writer. (See, you are not the only one who has to DO THE WORK FOR THEM!) You want to be in the position where you are that writer being recommended, so that is why, as we've mentioned in previous chapters, it's crucial to ingratiate yourself into a publicist's good graces from the get-go. The relationship can and will be symbiotic.

But don't always rely on THEM doing the work for YOU. Do it for them. That's your mantra, your golden rule, your #1 commandment. When querying magazines, send a cover letter that represents you and that stands out. In *Legally Blonde*, Elle Woods printed her resume on scented, pink paper. Is that silly? NO! Why? Because it stood out from everyone else's. In a world full of copycats, be an original.

Amy Says: When I was finishing up college, I did my cover letter as a press release on myself. I wanted to show magazines that I was applying to write for that I could write well and creatively, and since I was also applying for radio promotion and publicity gigs at labels, I wanted to illustrate that I could play the game, that I "got" the game, and that I was a creative, passionate thinker who went against the grain. I wanted to stand out. I wanted to win, and I showed that through my creative cover letter. I also did a press kit on myself. I cut the logos off the magazines, and took my best clips and made a press kit that looked like a band press kit. If I was sending the resume to Roadrunner, I made sure that clips I had written on Roadrunner bands were spotlighted in my press kit. It was a lot of work at the local *Kinkos* in Cherry Hill, NJ, but it got the job done. I got tons of interviews from that. Even label reps that I had minimal day to day communication with but had casual contact with over the years were impressed with my creativity, and forwarded my resume around their offices, thus helping me secure interviews. Case in point is the now-defunct TVT Records:

I had sent my resume to Anya, the college radio rep, whom I had dealt with while running my college radio station. I didn't talk to Anya every week, but I always sent her my play lists and dropped her a personal email once a month or whenever I received a TVT release, to tell her my thoughts and that I was supporting it with airplay. I didn't have any relationships with TVT's press department at that time, so I didn't send to their press department. However, when Anya got my resume, she knew that her company's PR department was hiring and forwarded it along. I got a call for an interview the next day. Because I had sent to someone I knew, rather than blind sending it when it was unsolicited, it got fast-tracked to the PR department. It was just smart business acumen. I also sent out clips to magazines. Some I never heard back from; others I did, picking up more freelance gigs.

In 2001 I interviewed for two jobs at Roadrunner Records after having turned them down twice for a job in 2000 because I wasn't ready to leave my cushy writing gig at *CMJ*. Irocically, I eventually ended up as a publicist in Roadrunner's press department, eight years after turning down the job, thus making me feel like this was the job I was supposed to be in. Even though the company had sought me out twice for jobs, because I had built such great relationships within the company and had supported their artists to no end, I knew this was the last time I'd be able to work for them. They wouldn't come back if I turned them down for a third time. I interviewed for the press and radio jobs. It was time for me to make the transition from college radio tip sheet to a label, to learn and to build my resume. And I could still freelance my ass off. It was the best of both worlds.

During the interview process I came up with creative ways to edge out my competition. After interviewing for the radio promo gig, I sent little radio shaped bubblegum dispensers to Mark and Dave, who were hiring for the job, with a note saying, "I want to get your artists on the radio!" After interviewing for the press gig, I mocked up fake New York Daily News covers, putting a picture of myself and the Roadrunner logo, saying, "Amy and Roadrunner: Perfect Together." I also put other headliners, like "Ill Nino Getting K-Rock Airplay" and "Slipknot Debuts At #2 On The Billboard Charts" to show them I knew what was going on at the label.

I got the radio job in 2002.

I got the press job in 2008.

By standing out from the crowd, Roadrunner came to me because as *CMJ*'s Loud Rock Editor, I made sure the label received premium real estate in my column and I would always make sure I let the promotion department know when I received a playlist that didn't "add" a Roadrunner release that week. I did the work FOR them. That's why they wanted me to be part of their team in house, as opposed to a supporter from the outside.

The whole point of this exercise? Stand out from the crowd. On my resume, I put a little picture of a chick with boxing gloves, to show that I was a tough cookie, and would battle for the company that I was going to work for. It always got mentioned in interviews. Because it stood out. I remember when the tables had turned, and it was me who was receiving resumes from contacts looking for jobs. While at CMJ, a music director at a college radio station sent me his resume and threw in a package of Ramen Noodles and said, "Please hire me so I don't have to eat these forever." You can bet your sweet ass I passed that along to my boss. Because it was creative and showed real initiative and a sense of humor. Who needs another boring resume with an "objective" printed on thick stock paper? Next.

Be prepared; responses don't always come quick. When starting out, you have got to realize and accept that you will not get a response. Even worse, you may get the one you don't want. Don't dwell. Move on. There are plenty of other companies/magazines out there that will want your talents. Keep seeking them out. Make them aware of you.

 Rick Says: I got the idea to start *Ruin Magazine* in October 2005. A mere four months after Metal N More had launched. I wanted my own metal magazine. I was tired of writing for other people's publications and only covering the bands that they wanted me to cover. Starting a magazine was actually easier than it seemed, in terms of process. Basically, I hooked up with a publisher through one of my contacts, and pitched the idea. The publisher loved the idea of a full-color glossy free metal magazine that covered the genre from "the extreme to mainstream" as I used to say, so I asked what the next step was. He told me I had to sell ads. Now, I asked, "How do I do that?" His response was something I will never, ever forget. He looked me in the eye and stated, "I don't know, you graduated college when you were 19, you tell me."

Selling ads for a magazine that didn't exist was not easy. All I had was a PDF of the cover and a dream. At first I would call up labels with this long spiel that I had written in my notebook. The speech was scripted and it basically described every aspect of the magazine. I instantly sounded like a tele-marketer, and I got turned down by about 50 potential advertisers that first month. I was so nervous cold-calling people. I would wake up at night with stomach pains because I was so nervous. It seemed like a failing proposition. I'd told everyone about the magazine, and it had become my life so I had to get it out. The only way to get it out was to sell ads, so you got it, I had to sell. I was used to the word "No" since I started hitting up magazines to write for them. I accepted that most people would say no, especially since I was still slowly making a name for myself. However, no one wants to hear those two letters together "N" "O." After trying and being denied numerous times, one day when I was making ad calls I forgot my notebook, which happened to have had my Ad-selling speech pasted in it. So I initially freaked, thinking "How am I going to do this without the script?" I just rolled with it. I struck up an actual conversation with the ad person. We talked about metal and comic books. Then I described the magazine and mentioned that we would be covering that label's bands. He was enticed, and actually asked me about advertising! I sold my first two ads that day, and I realized that the human connection will always beat a script. For as rigid as business can be, you need to hold onto that.

From there, things started rolling with *Ruin*. I began to hit up clothing companies and other outlets for advertising in order to diversify what we were doing. It eventually worked, and we got the first issue out. I stopped trying to be a salesman, and just acted as myself. Ultimately, that's what paid off, and it taught me numerous life lessons in the process. I managed to accrue that ad money over time, by being persistent. I'd craft short quick emails and give links to the cover and things snow-balled from there. I still heard "no," but that's the name of the game. All you need is the one person that's going to say "yes." Whether you're looking for a job, trying to write for magazines or trying to start a magazine, all it takes are a few "yes's."

You have to keep in mind that this is a fast-paced business. People have a lot of work to do. So keep your queries short and to the point. The more you ask for, the less you will get. Be precise with your requests to labels and magazines. Give a short intro and throw in some links to samples of what you've done. The best thing that you can do, if you are hearing "No" a seemingly inordinate amount is to keep trying. Keep writing and building your contacts. Maintain those friendships and also scour the internet for other opportunities.
Google and MySpace need to become your best friends. Everyone is on the Internet these days, and if you're looking for magazines, web sites, and labels to work for, search high and low. Even though so many people have said no, there are bound to be those that will say yes. Sometimes it's tough to be positive when you are so adamant about working in the music industry, and you have no contacts and doors aren't opening. However, keep smiling and stay focused.

Rick Says: I moved out to Los Angeles at 19 not knowing a soul. I hit up every film studio and company that I could find using sites like *www.entertainmentcareers.net* and *www. craigslist.org*. Eventually, I got in with New Line as an intern, and that proved to be the foundation for my whole career. You have to hit up EVERYONE that you can. Like Amy said, "Get used to 'No,' but don't just accept it and settle for it." There's a spot for everyone in the music world that wants to be here, you have to just keep trudging on. All you need is for one person to respond and take an interest. So never stop trying. Sometimes a little bit of extra effort is all that it takes to make a big splash.

IN SUMMATION: You will hear no, approximately 700 million times. Now's a good time to get used to it. Don't just accept a negative answer, keep trying and trudging onward.

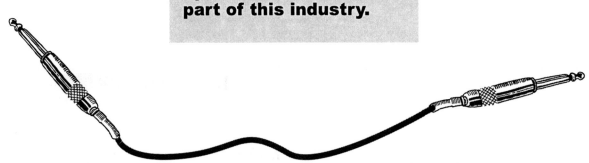

BOTTOM LINE:

Just so you can start getting used to it, we're going to say it once more so it sinks in:

"NO!"

Now that you've got that squared away, all it takes is one "yes" to build a foundation.

Once you hear that "yes," make the most of the opportunity.

"YES!"

- you can become a part of this industry.

Write Like You Have Never Written Before

CHAPTER V

Write constantly. Write in your journal, write on your computer, and write on bathroom walls if you have to. Spread you name and your thoughts. Even if you don't want to be a "writer" per se, general written communication is a huge asset to any and every company. You wouldn't believe how many capable, qualified people get turned down for jobs because they don't use spell check; because they interchange "they're" with "their" and "it's" with "its." Written skills can be honed. You don't have to be Shakespeare, Nabokov, Bukowski, or Melville. You just have to write well, write clearly, and be able to get across the points you want to make.

Basically, just being able to write is important. So practice. The best way to practice is to always write well. Don't even half-ass casual IMs and emails; constantly pay attention to grammar. So write correctly and professionally all the time. Instead of developing a shorthand for yourself, which may become so ingrained that you slip up when emailing a contact about a job or working together, always pay attention to syntax, grammar, spelling, and repetition. The best way to do that is to read absolute everything that you write out loud. When composing an email, read it aloud a few times, and make sure that it sounds professional and that it flows well. You also want to be sure that you don't mix up the person's name or company when emailing jobs. Be sure to use that wonderful marvel of modern technology known as "spell check." It's user-friendly and you should always use it before you send an email, a document, etc. Also, use punctuation, capitalization, and proper grammar. In the age of emailing, MySpacing, texting, and general written electronic communication, no one uses full words or proper techniques. So it's best to get into the habit of making things correct and uniform. Once you do something for a few weeks, it'll become part of your routine and you'll do it all the time. That means less chances for being sloppy or slipping up.

Amy Says: I am sure Rick will concur here, but there are two rules to being a good writer: First is that to be a better writer, you have to be a better reader. The second is that you are probably a better rewriter than you are writer. Don't just read magazines about the genre you like best. Read everything in the entertainment field. Read *Entertainment Weekly*. It's the best written, most comprehensive, and most satirical magazine out there. The writing is fantastic, and you will pick up plenty of new, usable words that don't feel plucked from a thesaurus. I used to carry around a tiny spiral notebook in my handbag and I used to "cull" words from *EW*, where I would write down words that I liked, that I didn't know the meaning of, or words that were strong. I then learned the meanings, and kept them in my brain for future use in my own writing, to make my own writing stronger and my vocabulary more vast. I pledged to use the word seamlessly in a sentence. Sort of like Cher in *Clueless* when she is trying to teach Tai to have a better image. But be careful when doing so. You don't want the word to be plopped in and incorrectly used. Again, it's all a part of becoming a better writer through being a better reader, and that includes reading your OWN material. Editing is a powerful thing. So don't be scared about spewing thoughts on to the page at first. Just do it. Get it out. You can cross shit out and rearrange things later. You can rewrite later. Just get the critical thinking out first.

Rick Says: Be sure to always be on your game. When you're just starting out, appearance is initially all you have. You need to appear professional. Composing clear and intelligent emails and resumes is the best way to do that. Below are examples of my current cover letter and résumé. I read this over numerous times, until it was perfect. That's the only way: read it out loud. You need to hear it, especially after staring at a screen for so long. So constantly pay attention to what you're writing. Even when texting your friends, because if you make a conscious effort to write coherently all of the time, it will show. You want people to know that you deserve their time. These days if I get a cover letter with a mistake from a writer, I don't even read their resume. It's just the name of the game.

Below is my resume from last year. Keep it short and simple. Make it concise, consistent and easy to read. Your resume should never be more than one page, unless you're Bill Gates. When you have 13 years of experience, then you can have a two or three-page resume. But when you are starting out and no one knows who the hell you are, stick to a single page and make it important. Below that is my cover letter. Both are concise, direct and easily modifiable to any, and all, job situations to which I might be applying. All these elements are very important when looking for a job in this industry, because as we went over, you're going to hear "NO" a whole hell of a lot.

RICHARD J. FLORINO III // Email Address
ADDRESS
PHONE

Professional Experience:
ARTISTdirect.com – Los Angeles, CA
Dec '07-Present
Editor
- Conducted interviews with marquis artists and high-profile film talent for one of the largest music web sites on the Internet, ARTISTdirect.com.
- Wrote CD and movie reviews as well as feature stories.
- Oversaw a staff of freelance writers, edited their work and regulated content production.
- Interviewed the following talent for exclusive features: John Travolta, Reese Witherspoon, Samuel L. Jackson, Chris Rock, Adam Sandler, Will Ferrell, Snoop Dogg, Slipknot, Staind, and Fall Out Boy.
- Supervised the creation of custom content promotional pages.

Citysearch.com – Los Angeles, CA
Sep '06-Nov '07
Manager of Merchant Content / Celebrity Content
- Managed a team of writers that created advertising profiles for Citysearch customers.
- Wrote ad profiles for businesses ranging from restaurants to night clubs.
- Conducted interviews with celebrities and musicians for online features about favorite celeb restaurants and spots across America.

Ruin Magazine - Los Angeles, CA
Jan '06–Jan '08
Creator / Editor In Chief
- Founded and created Ruin Magazine, a full-color, glossy, national heavy music magazine. The magazine had a circulation of 10,000 and was distributed nationally in more than 600 Hot Topic stores.
- Interviewed prominent artists for feature stories, photographed bands live and in the studio, wrote CD reviews, sold ad space, coordinated distribution, directed layout design, hired staff, and edited each issue of the 84-page magazine.

Freelance Writer / Photographer - Los Angeles, CA
Jun '05–Present
Revolver Magazine/ LAX Magazine/ BPM Magazine / Thrasher Magazine/ Metal Edge Magazine
- Contributed interviews, concert reviews, photographs, and CD reviews for *Revolver*, *LAX*, *Hit Parader*, *BPM*, *Thrasher*, *Metal Edge*, and *AMP*.
- Regular contract work writing artist bios and press releases for Universal Music Group, Interscope Records, MySpace Records, A&M, Island/Def Jam, Roadrunner Records, Warner Bros, Emotional Syphon Recordings, Mitch Schneider Organization, Nitrus Records, Century Media Records, Mosley Music Group, and Koch Records.

UBL Recordings LLC - Los Angeles, CA
Dec '04–Mar '06
Product Management Consultant
- Assisted in concept and art direction for CD/DVD compilations, proofing artwork, and coordinating with the label's distributor Navarre Corporation.

New Line Cinema Corporation, Los Angeles, CA
Aug '04–Dec '04
Intern in Music and Development
- Broke down scripts for music cues, burned CDs, and executed other general office duties.

Education:
BOSTON UNIVERSITY - Boston, MA
Dec '04
College of Communications
Bachelor of Film Studies
Graduated Magna Cum Laude

Skills:
Proficient in Microsoft Word, Microsoft Excel, Adobe Photoshop, Macromedia Dreamweaver.

(Writing samples and references are available upon request)

Dear Recruiter, [Insert Individualized Name for Each Job]

My name is Rick Florino, and I'm interested in the position open. I have written for national print magazines such as Thrasher, Metal Edge and Chord since early 2005. Last year I started a successful full-color glossy heavy metal magazine called Ruin. Ruin is distributed nationally via Hot Topic, Newbury Comics, Bullmoose Music, CD Tradepost, Meltdown Comics, Evans Music City, Halloween Town, Sikworld.com and Star500.com. I also write biographies for record labels, bands, producers, actors and directors. My work includes pieces for: Roadrunner Records, Timbaland's Mosley Music Group, Nitrus Records, Century Media Records, Korn guitarist James "Munky Shaffer," Fear Factory guitarist Dino Cazares, DJ Uberzone, award-winning music video director Nathan Cox and many more.

In addition, I have been an Editor for ARTISTdirect.com since December 2007. At ARTISTdirect, I conduct interviews with marquis artists and high-profile film talent. I supervise the creation of custom content pages, and I oversee a pool of freelance writers. My interviews include pieces with John Travolta, Adam Sandler, Reese Witherspoon, Chris Rock, Samuel L. Jackson, Slipknot, Fall Out Boy, Snoop Dogg and many more. Due to my diverse experience, I feel I would be a perfect fit for your company.

At this point in my career, I am interested in focusing exclusively on writing. However, I want to branch out further as a writer, and I believe I would become an integral asset to your company. My unique writing style would certainly complement your publication.

Please let me know if we can set up a mutually convenient date and time for an interview. My resume is attached.

Sincerely,

Rick Florino

Amy Says: Below is my résumé. I have four résumés. I have a massive comprehensive monster with all of the stuff I've done over my career and then I tailor a résumé to each job for which I apply. Below is the "monster," which I would never send out to anyone. It just is the career-long tally I've amassed and I can cut and paste, nip and tuck for whatever purpose it needs to serve. I also keep this to remind myself of all the shit I've accomplished.

ROADRUNNER RECORDS: Record Label: NYC, NY
   National Manager Of Hard Rock Promotion (Jan. 2002 – Dec. 2004)
   Director Of Hard Rock And Regional Video Promotion (Jan. 2005 – Dec. 2007)
   Director Of Publicity/Artist And Media Relations (Jan. 2008 – Present)

*Quarterbacked all national hard rock radio promotion campaigns of all label releases to multiple metal and specialty formats; work with the Active Rock, Modern Rock, Mainstream Rock, Community, and College formats with metal/hard rock programming, securing heavy airplay for all my releases.
*Handled servicing and promotion of all hard rock releases to Canadian and Mexican radio.
*Maintained relationships through daily phone, email, and instant message contact with Program and Music Directors.
*Managed, devised and implemented promotions, including concert presentations, product giveaways, interviews, contests, station IDs, station visits, on-air performances, meet and greets.
*Achieved the #1 chart position and #1 Most Added position on nearly all of the artists/ projects I've Promoted, both heritage and up 'n coming. Key metal radio successes include Slipknot, Killswitch Engage, Hatebreed, Dragonforce, Trivium, Machine Head, Opeth, Coal Chamber, Devildriver, Soulfly, and Stone Sour.
*Built support foundations for countless baby bands.
*Rebuilt label artist relations with key specialty programmers.

*Planned strategic promotions around album release and album launches, thereby increasing record sales.
*Worked with the marketing, tour, and press departments to maximize album sales goals on micro and macro levels.
*Dealt with crises when representing the artists to radio programmers and vice versa; liaison between all my artists and nearly 2000 radio programmers/DJs and video show programmers/hosts.
*Oversaw, coordinated, and organized radio and video mailings to 2000 outlets.
*Manage the metal radio budget, write POs.
*Devised, implemented, and quarterbacked promotion of all label videos to national and regional video outlet.

*Reported directly to Senior VP and VP Of Promotion.
*Generate label press releases, sales and marketing copy, and band biographies.
*Make daily pitch calls to national, regional, online monthlies, weeklies, dailies.
*Make daily pitches to local and national television outlets.

*Secure placement and coverage of artists in national, regional and online outlets.
*Manage relationships with top-tier of editors, writers and bookers.
*Liase with local media, venues, promotion staffs.
*Maintain daily phone, email, IM, and MySpace contact with writers across the world.
*Write and post website news, write the popular "Ask Amy" column on
www.roadrunnerrecords.com.
*Organize mailings, press kits, and clippings.
*Coordinate relationships between 30 artists and over 2000 media contacts, managing crises and communication
*Pitch artists and cultural stories.
*Report directly to the VP Of Marketing and Senior Director of Publicity.

*Have supervised, trained, and worked with over 25 interns.

*Awards:
FMQB Metal Promotion Executive Of The Year:
2003, 2004, 2005, 2006, 2007
FMQB Metal Promotion Trendsetter Of The Year: 2005
FMQB Metal Label Of The Year: 2004, 2005, 2006, 2007

CMJ NEW MUSIC REPORT: Weekly industry trade: NYC, NY
Loud Rock Editor (Aug 1998 – Jan. 2002)
Freelance Loud Rock Editor (July 2002 – January 2008)

*Wrote, edited, and laid out the Loud Rock section: reviews, features and hard industry and artist news.
*Coordinated playlists of Loud Rock radio stations.
*Acted as the liaison between label promoters, publicists, radio stations, bands, and management firms in the hard rock community, disseminating information from commercial, college, local, and national sources
*Researched, developed and created Loud Rock Crucial Spins, a spins-based airplay chart, which established never before held relationships with a panel of key commercial radio stations.
*CMJ Music Marathon (annual convention): Set up all Loud Rock programming panels, selected bands to book for showcases, and moderator and scheduled Loud Rock panels from 1998 through 2005.

SIRIUS SATELLITE RADIO: Satellite Radio Network: NYC, NY
On Air Talent (Oct. 2003 – May 2005)
*Hosted a 6-hour metal radio show on Saturday and Sunday nights, recording 4 news-filled breaks an hour.

*Have extensive knowledge and capabilities with the sound board, Prophet software, and Wizard Editor.

*Received dozens of messages and emails per week from listeners who tuned in specifically for my show.

2008 HARD ROCK GRAMMY SCREENING COMMITTEE: Santa Monica, CA
 Screener (September 2008)
  *Invited to be a member of the 2008 Hard Rock/Metal Grammy Screening Committttee

FREELANCE WRITING: Since 1995, I have written for *Kerrang, Decibel,* Spin.com, VH1.com, *Guitar World Juice, Sucker, Rockpile, Amp, Hails & Horns, Ruin, Mean Street;* served as "contributing editor to *CMJ New Music Monthly,* and as both intern and assistant to the Metal Editor of FMQB.

BAND BIOGRAPHER: NYC, NY:
(Feb. 2000 – present)
  *Have written band biographies for many independent and major labels, including RCA, Warner. Bros., Epic, Island Def Jam, Arista, Roadrunner, Century Media, Equal Vision, Abacus, Fearless, Tooth & Nail.
  *Have worked extensively with the bands, A&R and press staffs to create informative bios to present the bands to various press, retail, and marketing outlets.

HIT PARADER: (Monthly, 100,000 circ): NYC, NY:
Editor (Feb. 2003 – present)
  *Plan, devise, and execute features and stories; assist with lay out, content, editing, and special issues.
   *Create new columns.
  *Work with advertising sales staff to generate revenue.
  *Report directly to the Executive Editor.
  *Maintain contact with the Art Director and freelancers, generating assets, collecting, and editing content.

ALTERNATIVE PRESS: (Monthly, 300,000 circ): Cleveland, OH:
Contributor (May 2006 – Present)
  *Compose features and pitch story ideas to Editor-In-Chief and Managing Editor.

www.beautynewsnyc.com (Web): NYC, NY:
Staff Writer (June 2005 – June 2008)
 Beauty Editor (July 2008 – Present)
  *Compose features and product reviews, pitch story ideas to section editor.
  *Maintain contact with product publicists.

AQUARIAN WEEKLY (Weekly, 100,000 circ): New Jersey:
Contributor (September 2004 – present)
  *Compose cover stories, features, live reviews, pitch features to editor, maintain contact with publicists.

OUTBURN (Quarterly, 60,000 circ): LA, CA:
Contributor (June 2004 – present)
> *Compose features and reviews, pitch story ideas to Editor-In-Chief, maintain contact with publicists

METAL MANIACS: (Monthly, 50,000 circ): New York, NY:
Album/Feature Writer (August 2002 – present)
> *Compose features and reviews, pitch stories to Editor-In-Chief, maintain contact with publicists.

CHORD (Bimonthly, 30,000 circ): LA, CA:
Contributor (June 1995 – present)
 Editor (January 2002 – present)
> *Compose features, pitch story ideas to Managing Editor.
> *Served as Managing Editor for the Summer 2006 Warped Tour Edition, choosing all editorial, assigning Stories, collecting stories, writing copy, copyediting, fact-checking.

ARTIST DIRECT.com (Web): LA, CA:
Reviewers/News Columnist (February 2008 – Present)
> *Review albums and movies, write 5 movie-related news stories per day.

REVOLVER MAGAZINE: (Monthly, 150,000 circ.): NYC, NY:
Senior Writer (April 2001 – May 2006)
*Created, coordinated, researched and wrote the death/black metal and hardcore columns, as well as other features and reviews.

DECIBEL MAGAZINE: (Monthly, 50,000 circ.): Philadelphia, PA:
Contributor (April 2005 – April 2006)
> *Wrote 5-page features and live reviews.

KERRANG MAGAZINE: (Weekly, 100,000 circ): London, UK: **NYC**
Contributor (June 2002 – June 2003)
> *Wrote 5-page features, cover stories and live reviews.

SPIN.com (Daily, 1 million circ): NYC, NY:
Contributing Writer (September 1998 – September 2000)

TEENPEOPLE.com (Daily, 1 million circ): NYC, NY:
Contributing Writer: (April 2003 – March 2004)

IN SUMMATION: When sending out your resume, make yourself stand out. (One guy sent a resume and a pack of Ramen noodles and said, 'Please don't make me eat these for the rest of my life! Hire me!' Amy sent out nuts with her resumes and said, 'You're nuts if you don't hire me!')

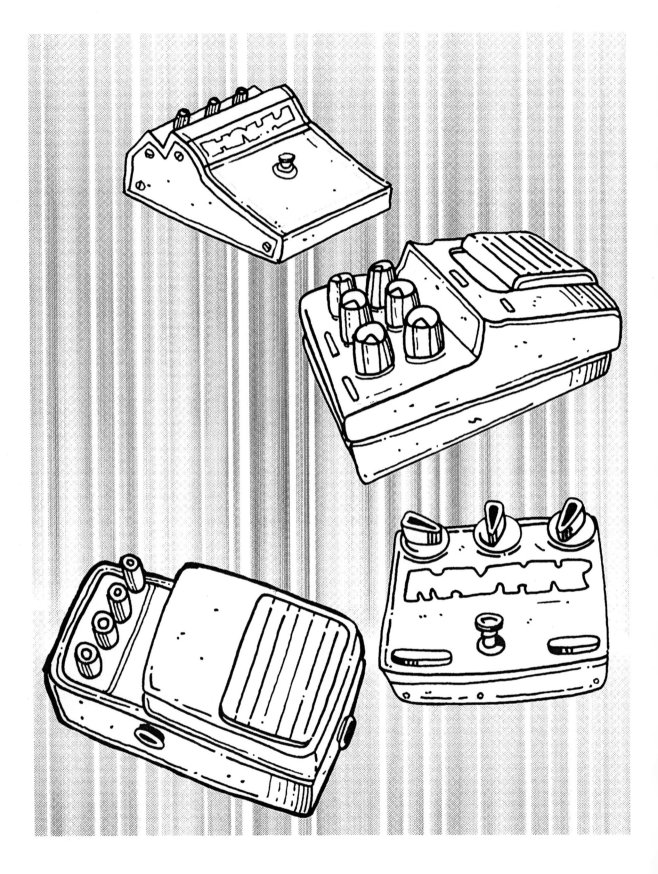

Interns:
Should Be
Seen and Not
Heard

(Workplace Etiquette)

As an intern you're there to get coffee and not fall asleep in meetings. That's the extent of your job. You're an intern. You work for free. Do not forget that. The janitor is in a higher company echelon than you are. He is also in a higher tax bracket. He also commends more respect. So keep your mouth shut, and your ears and eyes open. Now, even though you're working for free, you can still get fired, as we will recount shortly.

Now, being an intern is easy. However, most over zealous college kids make it hard. They don't realize that all they need to do to succeed is listen to their internship coordinator, ask questions, and complete the mundane tasks assigned to them with a smile. If you're interning at a record label, do not expect to be working with the band backstage. Do not expect the band to even acknowledge you. Chances are they don't know half the paid staffers. So leave them alone. Also, leave the executives alone. At most "industry" internships, the coordinator is usually an assistant or department head. That's the person you defer to. Listen to them and learn from them. If they ask you for coffee, make sure it tastes like you used to be a Barista at Starbucks. If they ask for copies, make sure they look better than Kinko's. If they ask you to answer the phone, you'd better answer it with a combination of Richard Simmon's pep and Al Green's cool. Always, always, always be in a good mood. You're lucky enough to be making copies and coffee at a record label. Cherish that opportunity and maximize it to its fullest potential.

Remember, this isn't supposed to be glamorous. Chances are, your supervisor started at the same spot you did. We all had to work up from there. Live with it, and start climbing the ladder, one rung at a time.

Rick Says: Now, I know this sounds repetitive, but it's as crucial as water and air. DO NOT FALL ASLEEP IN MEETINGS. It's very easy when you're in a toasty, warm conference room listening to a conversation you're not supposed to participate in, to drift off into dream land. However, given how "hard" your day is making coffee and making copies, you shouldn't be that tired. So be sure to stay awake in the meetings. Now, there are numerous ways you can do that. These usually last a long time. In fact the longest meeting I ever had was about six hours. Nothing important is EVER said in these meetings. Nothing is ever done. Everything said in a meeting could be accomplished via email. In fact, that would be far more efficient. However, they are a necessary evil of the corporate workplace, and no matter where you work, you will have meetings. I'm not going to lie, I have fallen asleep in my fair share. However, now that I'm getting paid, and I'm not trying to impress anybody, it matters less if I fall asleep.

The worst time I fell asleep in a meeting was at my first internship at New Line. I was so bored, and of course I adhered to the interns should be seen and not heard rule, so I wasn't going to say anything anyway. This meeting dragged on past the 90-minute mark, and I couldn't stand to keep my eyes open much longer. So I nodded off, totally lost control. BAD MOVE. About five minutes into my little dreamfest, a pencil hit me in the side of the head. It was my intern coordinator, a.k.a. my Boss. I had started to snore. I quickly came to my senses, and remembered where I was. He did not look happy. However, no one said anything until we got into the elevator and one of the executives exclaimed, "So Rick, did you have a nice nap?" I just chuckled, and that was it. It could've been avoided with a sugar-free Red Bull or some coffee. Those are both fixtures in any American office. Become friends with the deli or hot dog vendor downstairs, and he may even give you free red bull.

Interns, by definition, are in the office to do shit work. But if you keep your ears open and your eyes peeled, you will pick up on things that will help you better understand the business you have chosen to enter. So fine tune your ears, but don't eavesdrop. Be eager, but not annoying. You are there to learn, and you are actually paying, through your college credits, to be there, so make the most of it. Don't be angry that you're not getting paid. Because it is time to pay your dues out the ass.

Everyone remembers a good intern. So pay attention to your boss, don't be afraid to ask questions, even the dumb ones, and never, ever step out of line. Treat it like you are working in a bank, a *Fortune 500* company, or any place of business where professional business decorum and acumen are high priority. It may be a fun place to intern, but it's still a business. If you walk into the office all starry eyed at the platinum plaques on the walls and if your knees buckle when Insert Name Here is in the office for a press day, then you need to curb your fanboy/fangirl attitude and fast. No one may love the music or the business as much as you, but don't show it. It makes you seem like a kid who stumbled into a cool thing to brag to your friends about, not a hungry, pre-professional looking to bust through the door. The bands and the coworkers will never respect you if you are acting like the ultra uber fan. You are not entitled to anything. Once you accept that, you will make the most out of your internship.

Amy Says: I have managed over 30 interns in the course of 10 years working in the business. Some were fantastic, and of hiring quality. Others were abominations who gave great interviews when they came to apply for the internship but ended up doing lousy work. Others were abominations who gave great interviews, good resumes, did high caliber work, and yet couldn't function in the professional office environment. When I had to "fire" interns–and I used the quotes since it's hard to fire people who aren't getting paid—I had to tell them what they did right, what they did wrong, and that I had to let them go because their behavior reflects on me, and I can't have their actions making me look bad. I also can't give good recommendations to people who don't do stellar jobs.

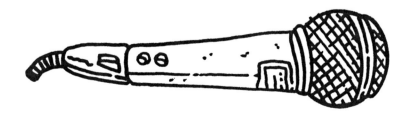

Rather than recount all the interns and to protect the not-so-innocent, we have come up with a handy list of things "not" to do as an intern. These are your 14 Commandments. We do not recommend breaking them, or even half-following them.

1 **Never make your boss look bad.**
Always make your boss look good.
When around other employees, follow the lead of your boss. Do whatever your boss asks. Don't disparage your boss. Don't question your boss. Always smile when around your boss.

2 **Never make yourself look bad.**
Always make yourself look good.
If someone else gives you a task, check with your boss, and then do it with a smile.
Make yourself indispensable, but don't appear to be a climber.

3 **Never go over your boss's head. This is a classic.**

Amy Says: I once had an intern who did great work: thorough, neat, orderly, and excitedly. But this intern, like so many of us, had rock star dreams, and wanted a back stage pass to OZZfest. When told, "Sorry, most paid staffers don't receive such credentials" and that "only the band's publicist and radio rep get the AA passes because of their DIRECT dealings with the band on site at the hectic all day fest," said intern didn't like that answer and went to OTHER people in the company, despite only having been on the job for a week or two. He hatched plan to get a pass, despite being told he was not eligible for such. At said OZZfest, he finagled his way backstage and proceeded to be loud, boisterous, and making a scene about his presence backstage. Employees noticed. Bands noticed. And he was promptly fired.

4 **Never speak out of turn or act up in the**
office or at company events.
This includes concerts, parties, dinners, etc. Do not try to be the center of attention.

5 **Always dress well at your internship.**
You want your boss to know that you take this seriously. Even though it's unpaid, act like it's more important than getting paid, because at this point you need all the contacts that you can get.

6 **Never do a shitty job.**
If you are asked to alphabetize a box of old press clips, don't say to your boss, "I haven't complained yet about doing this tedious job, have I?" (This actually, happened, says Amy!) That, in and of itself, is a complaint. Remember, there is someone else willing to do that same shit work for free. So don't give your boss a reason to replace you with someone else. Don't criticize the tasks you've been given; shut up and do them. No one said this shit was going to be glamorous. In fact, it's the antithesis of such.

7 **Never try and kiss ass with executives.**
It's like wearing a flashing neon sign that says, "I am new, green, and young." Execs often

require staffers to make appointments with them, so don't think you can just walk up to a VP and extend a hand. If a VP comes up to your desk and says, "Hello," then engage in the conversation with him or her. But don't go knocking on the door. Have your boss make the introductions.

8 Never say things like "I am the lowly old intern."

Say something like, "Hi, I work for Amy. This is my first time interning, and I am learning a lot." Stay positive even if you are totally drowning and not sure what you are doing. Most people aren't really interested in the answer when they ask "how are you?"

9 Never make a spectacle of yourself.

"I (Amy) once watched an intern"—not mine, thankfully—"punch an employee, because he got fall down drunk at a band showcase." That is the "no-no" of ALL "no-nos" and if you commit such an offense, you are an idiot meant to be a fry cook, because you can't handle yourself, your liquor, or being responsible for yourself. From there on in, he was viewed as a nutcase and his previous friendly exchanges (had he adhered to most of the commandments here) turned quickly cold and awkward.

10 Never overestimate your role.

"I (Amy) watched interns actually argue over who the 'lead' intern was out of the pack of interns working one summer. True, they were all high-caliber workers with great ethic and talent, but to watch them argue over who was the mack daddy of the interns was comical and laughable." Guess what guys? You're all the same level; you're all unpaid interns that can be easily replaced with a phone call to the local college career placement center. There is no lead intern. You may be the BEST intern, and all interns should strive to be the best, but you're all on equal footing. None of you gets a paycheck and none of you are irreplaceable.

11 Never confuse being an intern with being an employee.

This ties in with the above-referenced commandment, but seriously, remember that you are not an employee and you shouldn't be reading confidential documents you see left on the printer, reading the employee handbook in public, be listening on conversations and be obvious about it, be playing air guitar at your desk and cranking music at your desk, running up to executives who are obviously in the middle of a heated conversation, calling your friends on your cell phone and asking them to talk to such-and-such band that is visiting the office to meet with the staff, be telling staffers, no matter how friendly you become with them, about your sexual exploits, be coming back for a visit and telling the new intern sitting at your old desk, "So, you moved my posters? Who do you think you are?"

"I (Amy) watched every single one of these offenses committed by interns under my watch. At first, I was embarrassed by their bad behavior; then I realized they made themselves look like fools, but that didn't stop me from reprimanding them for conduct unbecoming of an intern." Don't be a fool. Don't think you are a rock star. Don't go around saying, "I could do a better job" than a staffer. That's disrespectful and way too cocky for your own good. Just show that you can do a good job and should be hired.

12 **As Ludacris says, "Don't act a fool."**

Don't be the person people remember as the "creepy intern." If you make a nuisance of your self, other employees won't want to have you help them complete a task, even when you are available to. You want to be remembered fondly, missed for the excellent quality of your work, and most importantly, recommended for a job in the future. So make the most if your time in the thick of things.

Remember, it's temporary, it's not a job, and it's a stepping stone to YOUR future.

13 **Newsflash...your first industry job is not going to be much different than your internship.**

Most entry-level assistant positions are the same crap, but you're getting paid. However, each level is a stepping stone and must be treated as such. Let's face it, you're not there to be an intern or an assistant, but as the old adage goes, "Everyone needs to start somewhere." That somewhere is the bottom. However, we've all done it. It's funny because now we both have our own interns, and we watch them go through the same rites of passage. It's like some *Herculean* test of strength and might, but everyone eventually makes it through. We're all better for it too.

14 **Work for a label.**

Start as an intern, as we mentioned no one will turn down free work—in fact, I'm willing to let one of you clean my apartment for free. Obviously New York and Los Angeles are the best places to work in the industry, but there are labels everywhere that you can get your feet wet. If you are in the middle of Bumfuck, Iowa, you can still intern for local radio, local print media, and make contacts, get free perks, and lay the groundwork for your paid future. It's always always, always about WHO you know. Taking classes or majoring in music business is nice and ambitious, but it doesn't mean jack compared to the kid who also spends 5 to 10 hours a month in an office environment.

BOTTOM LINE:

Photocopy this page!

Refer to the intern guidelines all the time.

They are your friends.

CHAPTER VII

Fall in Love With Networking

on't fall in love with the girl at the rock show; network with the girl at the rock show. There is time for love and fun later on. But for now, you've got work to do. Go to every show you can. Network with the photographers, writers, and anyone that's staff. Also, get to know your locals. We're talking radio DJs, radio programmers, and fellow writers. There is a ton of local media in your market. So make sure you are looking for it. Better yet, make sure you are making friends with those individuals who are representing it and are entrenched in it. These are called local resources, and you will learn to rely on each other.

There should be no limit to your networking size or your scope. Even if you want to work in the art department of a record label, still make friends with the mid-day DJ of the local radio station who you see at every show rocking out. The more people you know, the further you can get. Even better yet, you will meet some cool people along the way, people who will become your friends, and people who share the same interests as you. This business is not a job; it's a lifestyle, and you're not going to have the same life as your 9-5 working friends from college who hit the bar at happy hour and then go home and veg out. You will be constantly working and traveling in the same social circles as many of the people you meet. You may just be updating your website after hours, having dinner with a publicist, or meeting up with a local band after you leave the office at 7 PM, but it's still work. During the first few years, you are going to have a whacky, unconventional, and unorthodox life. That means things like dating and vacations will suffer. But it'll be worth it in the end.

Most of your friends will probably hate their jobs and eventually live their lives according to the rat race. You will never experience that emotion. Sure, the music and entertainment industries are competitive and tough to break into, but since it's such a cool business, you love it, and have a raging passion for it, when you finally do break in, you feel lucky to have that $24,000 a year job with benefits.. So accept that NOW that you will have to make large sacrifices. So, suck it up for now. Bite the bullet and let it knock out a few teeth; you can get those beautiful porcelain crowns and veneers later in life. But for now, hustle, bustle, and focus on your career. You will have time for life and love later. But remember, for the first 5 years, your job will become your life and that is how you become a player. Not a high stakes player, but a player on your own terms.

As for developing these contacts, be friendly. Be socially outgoing. If you have a hard time chatting and making small talk with people you don't know, then this will be an uphill battle for you. If you want to network and make contacts and connections, then you better be able to sell yourself through your social skills and ability to interact. Say hello to the radio DJs. Say hello to the photographers. Say hello to the tour managers. Exchange business cards. Offer to do some sort of cross-promotion. If you run a website, offer to exchange banner ads promoting their radio show and vice versa. It's all about one-hand-washing-the-other in this business and especially be sure to get to know everyone in your local market.

That includes the show promoters. Offer to give them some advertising, calendar space, or review space on your website in exchange for free tickets for yourself or tickets to give away to your readers. There's always work to be done together. Don't be shy, don't be afraid, and don't take your eye off the prize.

It also isn't a crime to make friends, and that term is used loosely, with band members, especially if they are local to your scene and you see them out all the time, although we do suggest you toe this line carefully. Many up-and-coming bands are young, excited, and happy to talk to and befriend anyone who is paying attention and supporting their band. That's ok. It's a give and take, symbiotic relationship. But sometimes publicists don't like when writers get too close to their artists, because then they lose control of the situation. So don't go flaunting that you have Joey Jordison's number in your Blackberry. You can keep email contact or even phone contact with artists, but don't harass them like you are best friends, either. Why? Because they're not. Remember, be diplomatic, toe the line, and don't develop a reputation as a stalker. Don't ask artists for their numbers right off the bat either. Use your caution and your discretion. You're not out to have a "hot" contacts list. You are out to further your career and to be trusted with sensitive info.

 Amy Says: I once contacted a band member that I had been friends with for 10 years. I am talking someone whose home phone number I have and whose family I have met. I was in a pinch and needed to fill column space in *Hit Parader* and was on drop dead deadline. I called said friend to give me a quote for the piece. He did it, no questions asked, based on our long term friendship. The next day, boy, did I hear about it.

His publicist, who had only met him three months before when she was hired on the project, called me up and bitched me out like I had never been before. She insisted that I had no right to go above her head and call the artist without her knowledge and - as the publicist, she would approve or deny all press requests. I told her to slow her roll; sure, I jacked protocol and did what I needed to do to meet my deadline and to give the band national press, but her reaction was overblown and a bit too 1988 for my taste. With print mags drying up, bitching out the editor of a national glossy is no way to nurture a relationship. However, there is a moral to the story. Don't go above a publicist's head if you don't have to, no matter what your relationship is to the artist. The PR rep may have contingent press and exclusives pending and you can't get in their way or then you can be grey-balled or black-balled down the road. So toe the line.

Remember, artists will appreciate all you do for them over the course of their career, so maintain a polite, cordial relationship with them post-interviews. If it develops into more and you attend their wedding down the road, great. If not, it ain't no thang, either. You didn't start your career to be their best buddies, and if you did, then maybe you should rethink your priorities and examine your motives.

IN SUMMATION: Remember who your friends are.

BOTTOM LINE:
Follow protocol.

Don't step on toes.

Diversify!

CHAPTER VIII

Today, there is one person doing the job that three people used to do at record labels, print publications, or radio stations. When less people do more work for more hours, because the pie has gotten that much smaller, everyone is still hungry. However, we cannot express the importance of diversification. The more you do, the more you learn, and therefore, the more marketable you become to future and prospective employers. . Never underestimate the power of being a journeyman. If you can pitch in and rise to the occasion of whatever situation you are tossed into, then you will get noticed quickly.

That said, if you love heavy metal, don't just write about heavy metal. That can be your niche when you're well-known, but don't turn down those articles on emo bands because you don't like them. Take on assignments about mainstream rock bands. It will be a challenge for you to write about things you don't like or aren't well-versed in. That will make you a better scribe, making you diversified. Sure, you love mac and cheese, but do you eat it for dinner every single night? No! The same theory applies here. You can have a calling card, an area of expertise, and a specific niche, but you also have to eventually grow up, grow out, and do more. A man of many hats is a valuable team player. If you start out in the press department as an assistant, don't scoff if the powers-that-be want to move you to the promotion department because they think you can fill a hole and become an MVP in another realm. Attack the challenge with aplomb.

Rick Says: Keep an open mind. Try any opportunity that's put in front of you. I didn't necessarily want to work as an assistant at an independent dance compilation label to start, but I did, and it was a good decision. Granted it wasn't my genre, but it was way better than working at a "regular" office job, and at that level, it provided a foundation for me that you'll learn at any label. . Plus, I was in Hollywood working in the music industry. That's more than most people ever do. To boot, I managed to write at night too and still hit every show that I wanted. What's most important is completely immersing yourself in the music, beyond what you do between 9am and 5pm. You really need to LIVE it and that involves putting music before everything.

It's worth it because once you become a part of the scene that you want to be in, you're never the same, and believe us, you'll never want to leave. So take that opportunity. Because everyone has to start somewhere even if it seems like it's a little different than what you'd expected. You will most likely be very pleasantly surprised.

IN SUMMATION: Study every kind of music you can and write about it. Never underestimate the value of DIVERSIFICATION. If you can contribute, be a team player, and can pinch hit in whatever situation you get tossed into, you will be the one everyone, including the mack daddy, notices. So, write for web sites. As the print market is drying up, websites are popping up. We live in the instant information age, and being current and scooping is much easier to do when you can post it immediately. Make yourself "the source."

BOTTOM LINE:

Keep an open Mind

Take absolutely every opportunity you're given

Run with it

Don't give up

Diversify your talents

Common Sense: Don't Leave Home Without It.

CHAPTER IX

We've already written that common sense is a hot commodity. It's also one of the main reasons we are writing this little tome. We've found out over the years that common sense isn't so common. Return to the intern chapter (Interns Should be Seen and Not Heard) for instances of releasing the intern into the wild—aka the office—and see how they were taken down by social Darwinism in a matter of hours!

Common sense isn't something that can be taught, so what you need to do is trust your gut instincts. If you are in a situation and your gut is screaming, then you should listen to it. Even if it's as simple as thinking this A&R guy you see out at every show doesn't dig you, then you should maybe limit your conversation with him. Say "hi" and "bye," but don't try and overcompensate or find out why he's giving you the brush off.

Furthermore, your gut reaction is also applicable to conducting interviews. If you want to ask a controversial question during an interview and you've got the subject in a great mental spot where he's spewing all sorts of detailed information that will make your story entertaining and readable, and suddenly your gut says "Don't go there, it may derail this train," then don't do it. Go for the reality of the situation if you've got the artist in a good place. Don't go for sensationalism. Don't ruin everything by asking a boneheaded, gossipy question. Use your common sense and go with your gut. If doing something doesn't feel right, it probably isn't.

If you think something may be a bad idea from the outset, trust us, it probably is. So be respectful of artists, label staffers, yourself. You don't want that reputation of being the annoying person who doesn't know how to have patience. Hitting people with continuous emails and calls isn't going to help your case; it's only going to annoy others. So, harness any neurotic tendencies you may have and don't cross the line from persistent to annoying, in ANY situation, whether it's following up on a job interview or following up on an interview request with a publicist. The music business surely doesn't run on our clocks and it won't be running on yours, either. Remember, in the ever-shrinking music business, less people are doing a lot more work. They are busy and may not be able to respond to your requests right away, so don't always assume the worst.

Don't be a pest or a mooch. One of the biggest faux pas we have seen the up and coming music biz'ers make is thinking they can bleed labels for product or tix. Asking your label contact for copies of jazz CDs that you only want for your personal collection but are never going to write about is rude and unprofessional. Don't ask your label contact for entire catalogs of bands they are not currently working with just because you want to impress your girlfriend. Don't ask for tickets to that boy band your contact is working with because you want to give your little sister a cool birthday present. Trust us, your reputation as such will spread like a flesh-eating virus to other labels, other publicists, and other contacts. So don't go there, unless you have a very long, very healthy, very established relationship with your contact. We have seen people run out of the business because their personal greed got the best of them and when they had legitimate assignments, the label staffer didn't want to provide promos because the trust with the writer had been eroded.

Conduct yourself like the professional that you are at all times. Don't let the perks of the job become your sole purpose. Do it for the love of music.

Rick Says: Respect and relationships are the two most important things in this industry. When you start off in this industry, keep an open mind and an open ear. My grandfather used to always say, **"You have two eyes, two ears, and one mouth."** It makes sense. You should talk half as much as you watch and listen.

As a first-timer at a label, management company or magazine, you do not know more than the people who have been employed there. Listen to them. Watch how they act and learn from it.

Ask questions, but don't repeatedly ask the same question. That's a mistake. Listen and pay attention to what your supervisor says in the first place. I used to carry a notepad around, because I didn't want to be annoying by asking the same things over and over.

I was nervous when I started my first industry job, because I really did treasure it. However, it's better to be confident and aware. That's part of the virtue of common sense. If you've been hired as an intern or an assistant, even it's your very first industry job; the company obviously believes you can handle the job. So ask questions, pay attention and be aware of your surroundings. If you need to take notes, do so. There's nothing wrong with copious scribblings on job tasks to remind you. It shows that you're astute and you care about each task. I still make itineraries for myself to break things down to a formula. Once you have a pattern or a schedule, things are a lot easier. This will help you become more familiar and confident with what you're doing and will aid in your success.

Furthermore, you should be aware of everyone's role in the company you're working for. You want to be familiar with what everyone does so you know where to go when you need help or have valid questions. And common sense will tell you to show all of your superiors respect as well. They've made it to the positions that they have because they once started off where you are. Remember, everyone's been an intern or an assistant at some point, it's a learning experience. So be aware and learn.

Now, back to my Grandfather's quote about having two eyes and two ears, it doesn't mean that you shouldn't talk. It means when you do talk, be aware of who you're talking to and what you're about. Use your common sense and your judgment for each situation. You probably wouldn't approach the president about the bathroom toilet being clogged. In fact, that's not even a question for the janitor, let a plumber know. It's a jungle out there and common sense just requires paying attention and remaining aware of your surroundings.

Amy Says: Since Rick and I had very wise grandparents, I'd like to inject a note of wisdom that my grandmother used to say that absolutely fits what Rick is saying. My grandmother used to tell me and my brothers, "Little children should be seen and not heard." It was her way of telling us to be quiet while she was watching "her stories," but what she really meant was that we should be visible and that people should notice what we did, not what we said. And so, my suggestion is to heed my grandmother's words. Your work and your work ethic will be what people notice. It's probably best to speak after you are spoken to, as well. So watch what you say, how you say it, and when you say it. Keep the personal chatter to a minimum. You can make friends with your coworkers, but keep the personal conversation off the clock and at the bar around the corner after hours. Likewise, don't be the quiet, mute weird guy at the office, and don't be that loud, obnoxious person that everyone thinks makes a spectacle of him or herself.

Those big gigs will come, but you've got to start somewhere. So take it slowly. Use your head and approach each task you're assigned with serious dedication. If you're set to do certain tasks, do them and excel at them. Then, let people come to you with more tasks. If you start overextending yourself in the workplace, people can sometimes become jealous; worrying you may be upstaging them.

Another important thing is to not step on anyone's toes. If there's a graphic designer in the office and you're the mailing intern, let your supervisor know you can do graphic design, and maybe do some stuff on your own to show your work. Don't approach other departments and try and tell them what to do; remember, you don't know better. You may think that you do, but you don't because there is always someone at the top who has more experience, more wherewithal, and more access to the budgets that are used to implement decisions. Once you get hired, then you can make suggestions and write memos or marketing plans and suggest changes you think might work.

Trying to act like you know better? We've seen that go awry as well. We have numerous experiences with know-it-alls that'd make your hair stand up. The best way to approach every situation is to use good old fashioned COMMON SENSE. Use those two eyes and two ears way more than your mouth and you'll go a long way. Be wary and remember everything you say will be remembered. Know your role and treat every moment at that first gig as a learning experience. You don't want to be remembered as "Ray, The Idiot Intern," because you asked an executive that you didn't know to add cream to your coffee.

You don't need a PhD to work in the music industry; you just need to be charismatic and savvy. We can't stress this enough. Your personality and your brains will get you everywhere in the music biz, so you need to have a combination of both. Be like the last surviving cockroach after a nuclear meltdown.

Lastly, and this is something you should have mastered in kindergarten: always say "please" and "thank you." We both use those two simple phrases when we talk to superiors, peers, and interns. Get in the habit of doing that now. It goes a long way.

Common courtesy is just as crucial as common sense. You can show your enthusiasm, reliability, and general passion in these simple polite exchanges.

IN SUMMATION: Use your head. Common Sense is your best friend.

BOTTOM LINE:

Common Sense pays off.

Be aware of your surroundings.

Be aware of who you're talking to.

Be aware of departmental divisions.

Excel, but don't step on anyone's toes.

Use your two eyes and ears to listen, watch, and learn.

Don't repeat questions.

Carry a notepad or take notes on your handy dandy blackberry in between sending nifty text messages to your friends about how cool your industry job is.

THE OLD SWITCHEROO

(Be Able to Change Jobs and Remain Versatile)

CHAPTER X

It's interesting the way things switch around in this business. You may go from magazine writing and working with publicists to becoming a publicist, or vice versa. The great thing about the music business is that you can have a chance to see both sides of the coin and your versatility will make you that much more employable down the road. And each and every experience and job will shape your future in some way. If it doesn't, find a new gig. Once you stop learning, stop thriving, and stop being enthralled by your daily duties, it's probably prime time for a position or company change. Don't forget that you've worked your way up and now you've got a 401(K) to think about.

Rick Says: I've worked a whole hell of a lot of places. I interned at New Line Cinema in their music and development departments. I worked full-time in the New Line Cinema mailroom. I also was an assistant at an electronica label that produced dance music compilations. Then, I became an editor at *Citysearch.com*. I wrote about restaurants, bars, clubs, salons, insurance agents, plumbers, electricians, and just about every other Yellow Pages category that you can imagine. I also handled celebrity content for them, and I got to interview various Celebrities about their favorite places to chill and dine. Each day my job got better and better, bringing me closer to becoming a writer full-time which is what I wanted to do. However, during my interning at New Line to writing at *Citysearch*, I freelanced for metal magazines, did bios for record labels, and ran a full-color glossy metal magazine in my free time. I filled my free time with a second full-time job, and that was really a lifestyle choice. Now the hard work has more than paid off and I get to write about music all day at ARTISTdirect. com. My passion became my job, but it was worth it and each gig beforehand served as a stepping stone.

Working at a label you learn the ins and outs of the industry, even if you are only entry-level. I learned about publishing, licensing, day-to-day label functions, inventory, signing artists, and much more. It's all the same at every label in terms of process, regardless of the genre. So even my first job working for an electronica label served its purpose.

Working in the music department at New Line opened the first doors in the industry for me and I got to see how a big film studio's music department worked. This all happened while I ran *Ruin Magazine*, in my free time. I learned both sides of the industry. I learned the label and the creative writing side. Plus, I managed to build a huge social network. Each interview gave me insight into how the bands lived and worked, and as a result, I now have a solid view from both sides of the coin. This helped when I seamlessly went from running *Ruin* to managing an editorial staff at *ARTISTdirect*. And it's all because I'd gained experience in every facet of the industry when opportunities were presented to me.

So whether you have the chance to start off at a label, a magazine, or another part of the industry, take it. Even if it's not your final passion, learn from it, because all of that knowledge will prove very useful for each and every following endeavor that you take on in the industry. It's all about building upon past experiences. There is nothing more valuable or enriching to your marketability and your hire-ability than well-roundedness.

cheesburger combo
no onions, no tomatoes *coke*

Amy Says: When I left my job as Loud Rock Editor for *CMJ New Music Report* to take the promotions gig at Roadrunner Records, it was extreme culture shock. It was the perfect gig for me, doing exactly what I dreamed about at the college radio station at Rutgers. I wanted to be the person who wrote the Loud Rock section. And I was. Bands used to call me "CMJAmy" and the gig was such a part of my identity that letting go and leaving it was the most difficult professional conundrum I had ever experienced. I still believe I was the definitive editor of that section and it is a part of my history, but now, with the clarity of 20/20 hindsight, it was what it was: my first job out of college and that which established me. Looking back, over seven years later, I can't imagine how miserable I would have been had I stayed there. Not because it was a bad job. I loved it, but it wasn't the only job I was meant to have if I wanted to be a well-rounded career woman. That's what happens when you grow up and change: everything looks different. Of course there was an incredible amount of separation anxiety because I loved what I did and it seemed like the perfect job for me at the time, but it was only the perfect job for a young heavy metal fan out of college who had carte blanche over what she wanted to cover. I had taken the column from two pages, three reviews, 500 words of news, and one chart to five pages, five reviews, and 1000 words of news, industry chatter columns, and two charts. I essentially doubled the size of the section, making it the most popular read in the mag under my tutelage.. (A side note: I was only off the job for five months. After five months, they came back to me and asked me to freelance the column, and I happily obliged. But things were never the same as they were when I was "CMJAmy" in-house.)

Today, leaving *CMJ* for Roadrunner was the smartest decision I ever made, and if I tried to leave Roadrunner, it would be a million times harder than it was to exit *CMJ*. The reason that decision was absolutely the correct one is not just because *CMJ* appeared headed for financial ruin at the time, but it was the essential choice because I needed to do something other than write. At Roadrunner, I could have the best of both worlds. I could write for as many magazines and work with the best metal bands and labels in the business. I was able to straddle the line between both worlds without a net and I never lost my balance. I was able to work my tail off, promoting the bands and getting them on the radio, and develop relationships with the bands on a much deeper level than I had as a writer on the outside. I was able to look at multi-million dollar budgets and how they were allocated to specific resources in the company for specific purposes of trying to break the bands. I was able to see how the press department ran from the inside and when the department lost a member, I was recruited to write the press releases and bios and to make pitch calls while they were interviewing the replacement.

Eventually, I was asked to also handle video and TV promotion at Roadrunner. That expanded my world of contacts tenfold. I had radio, video, TV, web, and print contacts. Many of the writers wanted to talk to me because they were familiar with my work as a journalist, and also wanted to ask for my advice. That made it easier to transition when the company decided my skills would be best suited in the PR department. The move was less rocky than I expected, simply because I had written for every national glossy metal magazine and had relationships with editors and writers from my journalism career, so it's not like I was new and without contacts. I kept moving and growing within Roadrunner to the point where I bled Roadrunner Red (the color of our logo). I have broken bands, seen my efforts translate to record sales. Most importantly, I aided in finding music its audience. And the best part was that I had remembered wanting to do that when I was 17. I saw people I did not know, when I was in my room in West Collingswood Heights, New Jersey, listening to Snapcase, Earth Crisis, Deftones, Hatebreed and Misfits. The opportunity to do this myself is a result of the skills and experience I'd gained from being versatile throughout my career.

The point of the old switcheroo story is that in any facet of life, if you stay in one place too long, you will stop growing and will become content. It's easy to stay where you are, but if you show the willingness to grow, to expand, to try new things, and to take one for the betterment of the team, then you will be seen as the ultimate, invaluable team player. You will have a leg up on the competition because you can do more and handle more. Demonstrate that. If you have proven that you can take on new tasks with a smile, no matter how non-glamorous they are, then you will be golden. Multi-taskers and journeyman have become more valuable than overpaid executives in this version of the music business. And this is helpful today because the model is changing since everyone gets their music for free now, which is making the labels less and less relevant. So evolve, or the jackals will be feasting on your carcass once the lions are done with it.

Moreoever, don't over personalize your job or your position. So suck it up, forget about how "personal" and "identity defining" your job is to you. It's a lifestyle and it's a career, but in all reality and actuality, it's just a fucking job that you are incredibly good at. They say it is impossible to serve two masters, but that's hogwash. You can and will serve two masters. You can excel and become an expert in many fields within a single company simply by taking on tasks and keeping your ears open in the workplace.

But remember, versatility doesn't mean you are allowed to eavesdrop on conversations that don't concern you, especially as an intern. If the licensing department is discussing a band's royalty rate or how their option on the next record is most likely not going to be picked up, don't tune your ear to that. It's not your business and if you are not considered 10000% trustable at the time, then you could have your internship cancelled or dismissed because you are a risk to blab sensitive company info. Instead, if two colleagues are discussing a sales plan or a retail marketing attack, maybe ask some questions but don't slyly or sneakily insert your way into the conversation. Casually ask a fellow coworker or someone you work with if you can attend a meeting where these things are discussed. Instead of eavesdropping, live and you'll learn.

Speaking of versatility, if you like to write but there are no in-house writing positions, take a job in the PR department, where diffusing bombs and putting out fires is the main job. But to do that effectively, you have to have excellent communication skills, and that is where your writing background comes into play as an asset. If you can get your point across to the media efficiently and effectively, then you will have an easy time. In fact, if you take a label or management job and can't write because it is seen as a conflict of interest, use a pseudonym. Fake your name and your byline, as long as that's not going to get you fired or in trouble with your bosses. There are ways around it, and you can get it done. We promise.

Don't turn down a task or a project because you aren't interested in it or because you think it's beneath you. If the Digital Marketing department wants to discuss some new web initiatives and objectives with you, and you are a publicist, then sit down with them. Don't say "no" because you don't give a shit about this new email program feature they've enabled. Do it. Embrace it. Take notes. Learn. Try their suggestions. Ask them to teach you how to create an RSS Feed for your Google. Work with them. Take their advice. It will only make you more well-rounded and knowledgeable and as the music business goes barreling on, you will be equipped to survive the fallout. Become as technologically savvy as you can; you don't need to be the King or Queen of IT, but you are best serving yourself to know how to customize emails, how to hyperlink in a document, and how to organize your email contacts efficiently. Taking suggestions from your local, friendly IT guys is easy to do and necessary.

So there you have it. Be able to move around. Be a team player and a pinch hitter. Most of all, don't ever complain. Do it with a smile. We can't emphasize it enough. This is rock 'n roll. If you're not enjoying the ride, then there is either something wrong with you, you are lacking a pulse, or you just don't have the "it" that is needed to survive this business. The music business is changing, so if you can evolve with it, then you will outlast them all.

IN SUMMATION: Move around and you'll move up.

BOTTOM LINE:

**Learn.
Grow.
Evolve.
Be Happy.**

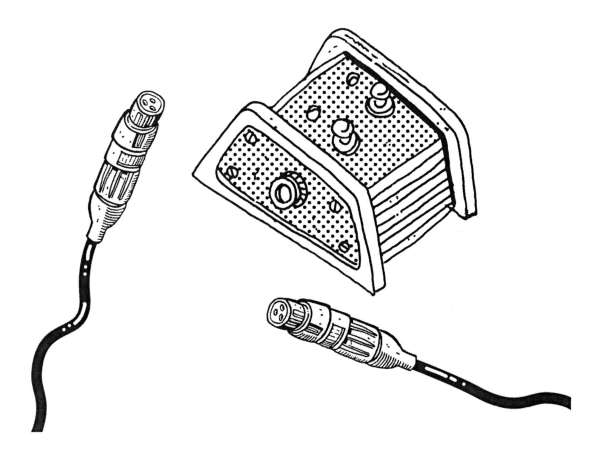

Start Your Own Business- Label, Magazine, Etc.

CHAPTER XI

Starting, funding, and running your own business is a frightening thought. Everything rests on your shoulders. But come on! You're capable. Think about how rewarding it will be to pay for your own health insurance, your own salary, and not have to answer to anyone but yourself. Even today's most successful label owners and magazine publishers started out working for a boss or for a multi-national corporation. Many of these industry leaders were forced to create their own business in order to keep themselves in the music business whether they'd been laid off, were fired, were forced to part ways, were downsized, or severed ties with their respective employers on their own terms. If you've listened to all of our suggestions, then you've made yourself well-rounded and picked up enough knowledge and experience to work for your own damn self by choice, not for the man. It's a risk, but with great risk comes even greater reward, so get to it.

If you want to start your own record label, first you'll need to find a band that you love and want to invest the resources in. Then, get all the facts and figures. Find out how much it costs to press a record in bulk, how much a designer needs to be paid for artwork, and how much it's going to cost you to print each album.

If you want to start your own management firm, find out how much being a manager entails—which is basically everything from arranging tour buses to approving interviews. That also includes the 5 AM calls from an artist that has missed his or her flight and needs you to rebook them or reseat them, pronto.

If you are going to make a pitch to a label to buy advertising for your print mag or your website, don't shoot off an email saying, "want to buy an ad?" You need to make a pitch that is well reasoned, and well written. Create a professional-looking PDF of a media kit, which has the rates for an ad and that has your circulation statistics, so that the label can see in hard, quantifiable numbers, what they are getting when they pay for advertising. Otherwise, you'll look like a piker and amateur. And it's 2009. The Internet, Photo Shop, and Adobe are your friends. Nuzzle up to them. Learn and love them.

The point of these exercises is to know what you are getting yourself into. Research the facts and figures. Drop a line to small labels or managers and ask them how they got their start. There's a wealth of information out there if you just know where to find it.

Rick Says: Starting your own business is not that hard and is pretty cut and dry. I started *Ruin magazine* when I was 20. All you need to do is utilize your contacts that you've built up, be prepared to work like there's no tomorrow, and be prepared to follow through. As I've said before, this has to become your life. Granted, it's your creation, so it should be fun. Just ask someone that's done it. If you want to start a magazine, ask someone that's already done it. If you want to start a record label, ask someone that's done it. If you want to start a management company (you got it) just ask. Most people will be happy to give you advice. Everyone in this industry loves to tell their "story." People will always talk about how they did it, and the best thing to do is to listen and learn from them. Let them inspire you and you may even find yourself a Yoda-style mentor. Sometimes that's all it takes too, old fashioned inspiration.

Here's a simple breakdown of how I started Ruin Magazine utilizing my contacts and fulfilling each need.

IDEA = I want to start a magazine.

Step 1 = Find someone that's started a magazine and ask them how

Step 2 = Ask contacts for that person

Step 3 = Contact magazine publisher based on a friend's recommendation

Step 4 = Meet magazine publisher and ask him for his story

Step 5 = Find a publishing partner for the magazine

Step 6 = Get money to get the first issue out

Step 7 = Sell ads to get more money

Step 8 = Assemble team of writers, designers, and photographers (ask for friend references again)

Step 9 = Collect all assets from writers, designers, advertisers, and photographers

Step 10 = Design the first magazine, bring it all together

Step 11 = Proof the magazine

Step 12 = Print the magazine

Step 13 = Distribute the magazine

Believe it or not each step was really that straightforward, and built upon common sense. I relied immensely on all of the contacts and friends that I'd met and that's really how it's done. It's funny, I even met Amy through my first publisher on *Ruin*.

See? RELATIONSHIPS DO LAST A LONG TIME!

IN SUMMATION: Start your own business – You got the label or magazine job, take it to the next level with your own thing. Even today's most successful label owners started out working for the "man" and then either got fired, laid off, parted ways, let go, or severed ties. That motivated them to do their own thing, to make their own way.

BOTTOM LINE:

Aspire to be your own boss.

Do everything outlined in prior chapters to get there.

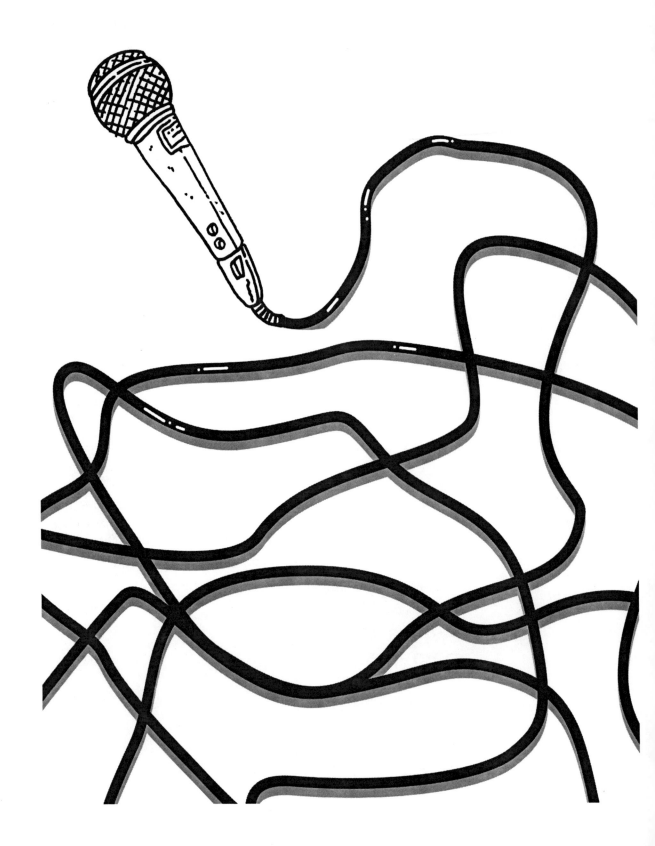

The
Solid

CHAPTER XII

The solid.

The solid is definitely not a bribe but it's also not quite a favor. In fact, we scratched our heads pretty hard when we sat down and tried to come up with a concrete definition on what a solid is. It's hard to define with a single example, but it's a basic operating principle in most industries and the most important thing we have to teach you in this book of knowledge. Essentially, a "solid" operates on the principle that one hand washes the other and I scratch your back, you scratch mine. It's the most symbiotic of all symbiotic relationships.

In its most general sense, the solid is when you go out of your way and do something for someone, with or without their knowledge, and you look out for them, do them a favor, without any benefit to yourself. It doesn't cost you anything and it's not a flashy or a flamboyant act. You don't do it to get anything in return. But chances are, even if you don't tell the person you did them a solid, they will somehow figure it out or know, and will repay the "favor" somewhere down the road. Could be years later. Could be hours later. The solid is something that will follow you in all of your music business travels throughout your life, and you will find it applicable in just about any business that you find yourself immersed or employed in. The music biz is obviously no exception.

If you are a writer, don't write back to a publicist only when it's about another band *you* need. Don't ignore his or her emails about their new project, and then only reply when you need or want something for an established act. If you only seek out or use your contacts in your time of need, then you can expect them to see you on the way down, and to not help you as you hit every single branch on the way down. You need to connect with your contacts daily, weekly, monthly and treat your relationship like a growing plant, one that requires attention. If you have them rely on you as well, you will have a fruitful, back and forth relationship. Remember the saying it's nice to be important? Well, it's more important to be nice certainly qualifies here. Be nice to that website writer –even if you cannot accommodate his or her request at the time- because he or she may one day be editing Billboard. You never know when you may need help down the road, so it's important to be civil and cordial as well, even in cases where you can't or won't look out and do a solid for someone.

 Amy Says: A concrete example of a solid is when I was the Loud Rock trade editor at *CMJ*. Whenever a label bought advertising in my section, I made sure to always give extra review coverage to the label. Obviously, they were not purchasing editorial from me, but I was just making sure to show them the love that they were showing me. By purchasing ads in my section, it ensured that the section operated at five full pages.

Also, when a label bought consistent advertising and there was a priority record "going for adds" for rotation at radio, I made sure to forward the label any charts that played the record but "forgot" to list it as an official add, so the label could quickly chase down that radio programmer for the add that they needed. I was looking out for them as they were looking out for me by supporting my section.

Another example of the solid refers to my ongoing relationship with Rick. I was writing for *Chord* for over ten years, when Gus, my editor, told me he needed me to write for *Ruin*, the new metal start up magazine that Rick was editing, to help get it off the ground. To have my name in it would give it an extra shot of cred, so I agreed, without any questions. I don't write for free, but I elected to do this for Gus because I had worked with him for so long. I had also struck up a quick and easy friendship with Rick and wanted to help him succeed using some of my clout. And look where we are at today. That small solid that I did – writing a few unpaid features on Stone Sour and Atreyu- generated a writing partner and a good friend.

Taking that gig from Gus was the best move I could have made..

However, doing solids doesn't always inspire reciprocity in others. A prime example is when I worked for *CMJ*, everyone and their uncle would come out of the woodwork during the *CMJ* Convention time, asking for a free badge. Those suckers run for $300, and you can bet your rump that they don't give 'em out for free. As an employee, I used to get a free badge and was able to provide three free badges to non-music industry friends. One year, a friend (I'll call her Jane) who had left the promotion business for the retail side of the business asked me for a badge. Now, keep in mind, I had been asked for about 100 badges at this point and had to tell everyone "no" because we didn't give those away for nothing. Turns out, another friend that I had registered a badge for had to back out of a 4-day convention in New York City, last minute. As a solid, I gave Jane the badge, and she told me that if I ever needed anything to just give her a holler. Turns out, she had tickets for a tour that I was dying to see and the tickets were scarce. I asked her for one ticket—not even a plus one—to the show and she basically told me that these tickets were impossible to get and she couldn't help me. In this situation, my solid ended up giving me a shitty return, but trust me, the benefits always outweigh the shitty experiences. In the music business, expect to do a lot and not have anyone pat you on the back. Expect to do solids that are forgotten about. But remember, those are the people who are going to fade away when you are rolling and are super successful.

Therein lies the difference. Someone who respects a relationship will bend over backwards to take care of you if you take care of them. It's wise for you to take stock of all the solids that people do for you and to consider them such. If someone gets you tickets to a sold out show and gets you great seats, remember that. So when you are in a position to give them an extra page of editorial or to give them great seats to a hot ticket, return the favor, even if it means you miss your express train home and have to take the local and waste an hour of your life.

Also, it's important to know that when you tell someone you are doing them a "solid" and then immediately expect a return favor, then it's not a solid. It's not a tit-for-tat situation. It's subtle, it's often unspoken, and they are never forgotten. It's a simple concept of looking out for people and it ensures that they will look out for you down the road. An old saying states, "There is no such thing as an unselfish deed." There's a real kernel of truth in that statement, and it surely applies to the music business. People who do good deeds are inherently selfish, because doing a good deed makes them feel good in addition to helping out someone else. And in the case of doing a solid, it's not about getting paid back in the here and the now. You are always going to be relying on your contacts, your connections, and your relationships to get your job done, whether you're a publicist, a writer, a radio DJ, a radio programmer, or a booking agent. It doesn't matter what exact job you are doing; you are always going to have to rely on others to help you achieve your end result, so it's best to nurture, foster, and care for those relationships as thought they were precious nuggets of gold.

No one likes someone who is constantly saying, "Look what I did for you." So don't make a spectacle when you go out of your way for someone. Be judged and noticed for what you do, not for what you say and not for how you say what you do.

There's that old Hunter S. Thompson quote: "The music business is a cruel and shallow money trench, a long plastic hallway where thieves and pimps run free, and good men die like dogs. There's also a negative side." No quote could be truer; the music business, like most entertainment businesses, is full of shallow, phony people who are out for themselves. We don't want to be those people and neither do you. Being a culture shaper and being someone who can dictate popular culture and can be a tastemaker is extremely rewarding, and we always must remember that we all got into this for our pure, untainted love for music. We should all be working together to keep it that way. Just remember: Always do solids. They almost never cost anything out of your pocket, save a little time. They are the very basis and foundation of the music business.

 Rick Says: The best way to get someone to remember you is to help them in some way. That goes for anything, really. Now, this whole business is predicated upon favors and people helping each other. Things have collapsed beyond belief because of downloading. That's the honest-to-God truth. Labels, magazines, web sites, bands, promotional companies and any other industry-related entity that you can think of are folding left and right, because the "pie" keeps getting smaller. Granted, of course downloading has been a part of that. However, it's also most labels' archaic perceptions of the business that have really led to the industry's collapse. Labels blow millions on frivolities: FedExing packages across the street, lunches in five-star restaurants, flying first class everywhere, and spending way too much to record. Unfortunately, with the advent of MySpace and iTunes, the communal aspect of music has dissipated more and more. Our culture has become completely isolated. We make individual playlists alone and have become glued to our sidekicks, iPhones, Treos, and Blackberrys. People don't buy music anymore, because it's not the communal thing that it used to be. Everyone used to buy the same Pearl Jam records and get together and talk about them. It was an event. Everyone went to the shows and hung out in the parking lot. There was a community before.

The Solid is one way to keep the human element going in the industry. Things cycle in this industry. One day, something's popular and the next day it's not. She's a fickle beast. However, as long as you're facing that with a willingness to evolve, you'll be fine. The labels are tanking, because most of the upper-corporate echelon don't know how to evolve. They're stuck in the old "hookers and blow" business mentality. That worked in the '70s, but in this day and age things have changed so much. There are no more "love-ins" in the middle of public parks with Jimi Hendrix playing impromptu. People commune via MySpace, Facebook, message boards, YouTube and technological means. We get way more text messages than calls. We don't even talk to each other anymore. It's not a bad thing, it's just reality. However, you need to play that to your advantage, because human connection is always necessary and it still goes a very long way. When you can hook someone up with something in person, in the "real world" it's meaningful, and even more than that it'll help set you up.

The only way that the industry will continue to live and breathe is for people to help each other. As the amount of money to go around has unequivocally become smaller, now more than ever industry-folk need to know that they can trust who they're working with. So you know what, hook everyone up that you can, when you can. If you can offer something to someone's cause and it doesn't necessarily break your bank and eat up too much of your time, why not help them? If you know a band that needs a contact at a label, and you've got that A&R guy's number, why not make the call? Your friend needs a publicist and you know music publicists, why not make that connection? Favors like that will go a long way, and even if nothing ultimately comes out of it, you didn't lose anything and at least you tried to help. Sometimes just trying is all it takes and making that little extra effort really tends to make a very positive impression on people. So when starting out in this industry where first impressions are all you've got, and for better or worse they will often shape someone's perception of you, coming across as willing to help out even a stranger will allow you to go a long way.

Personally, we've introduced bands to publicists, lawyers, marketing companies, record labels and anyone else that form our pools of contacts. Often, connecting people you've just met with contacts you trust, because you know that they will hit it off, is a gamble but it reaps rewards. Feel it out, trust your instinct and you'll know who you should refer to whom. Don't underestimate the power of those friendships and connections, because they will ultimately help you beyond belief. In this day and age, with the industry undergoing a serious change and evolution, you need to draw upon your contacts and connect them wherever you can. You want to be known as that beacon of positivity in this industry. There aren't too many of us. People do become jaded and disillusioned really quickly. That doesn't mean that you have to. Yes, there is a lot of hardship, disappointment and strife that comes along with breaking into and staying in this world. However, it's also the biggest rush ever to feel like you've accomplished something. You want to be a survivor and you want to make it. You need to stay positive to do so. If you're positive, even the most jaded of people will find that energy infectious and you'll make even more friends. This all goes to back to what we said prior: It's nice to be important, but it's way more important to be nice.

Amy Says: Through the years, old contacts have come to me, as well as neophytes looking to break in. Nothing is more satisfying than the emails I get from aspiring writers asking, "How do I get your career? You're basically my inspiration." It is flattering and everything I tell them, just as I tell you, dear reader, boils down to this: To be liked, be likeable. Always treat people the way you want to be treated. Never forget those who have helped you get where you are today. Because I have made this my golden rule, I have had Mike Boyle, who now works for R&R, a major music business trade magazine, interview me and feature me in a full page feature in the magazine, because he knows I've been entrenched in a scene for my entire career. I've been profiled on major websites and in print. I was contacted for an appearance on *Good Morning America,* which I am still waiting to follow through on!

You can get such treatment, too, if you do the right things. I will always write about music (much like I will always have a special place in my heart for my first love), but I have branched out and write about a broader range of topics now. In addition to music, I cover fashion and beauty trends. I write about tattoos for a rock magazine and an urban-leaning magazine. I was recruited for a major –and I mean major- blog endeavor that kicks off this year and I was asked to be the lead blogger on this household name based solely on the fact that "You're Amy." That meant a lot to me because I've spent many years building up an empire and a byline that brings the gigs to me. I am working on branching out into sports coverage, writing about baseball and football for league affiliate sites and I, too, have joined the movie world, covering movies with Rick at ARTISTdirect.com. I have become beauty editor at BeautyNewsNYC.com, covering cosmetics and beauty trends, because it's an area I've always wanted to get into and feel it can help me get to my eventual goal of writing investigative and trend pieces for *Vanity Fair.* I am also the Fashion and Beauty Editor for *LAX,* a gig that Rick lead me to, because, well, he practices what he preaches, so listen to him and to me! I am able to write about everything I love: music, movies, make-up and fashion. I like to be a tastemaker.

In the end, it's just a different branch on the same tree. If you are confident, follow all of the rules laid forth and lay your own foundation brick-by-brick, you will get where you need to be.

 Rick Says: The Solid is a foundation of career development. Because record labels knew they could trust me as a writer and interviewer, they began offering me the opportunities to write bios and press releases for their artists. I turned that into a lucrative side-business and got to further build my relationships. Magazines from *Revolver* and *Inked* to *LAX* and *BPM* have sought me out as a writer, just because my name had circulated around the scene and the internet. The most important thing that you have starting off is your reputation. To build a good one, you have to be willing to work with people and help them out when you can. Obviously, like I said before, don't go overboard, but if it's a phone call someone needs, or a little push for their record, or whatever, do it.

These days, I've segued into more film coverage, which I absolutely love, and the process is the same essentially—doing favors and showing extra attention gets you far. Within a year and a half of writing about movies, I've made friends with folks at every major studio, and I've gotten to talk to stars I've dreamed of interviewing like Samuel L. Jackson, Ray Liotta, John Travolta, Denis Leary, Hugh Jackman and many more as well as bands that I grew up idolizing like Metallica and Tool. These all came out in some amazing stories that you can read linked off of www.rickflorino.com. I'm also now the executive entertainment editor for *LAX Magazine.* They're the official full color, glossy magazine of Los Angeles International airport, distributed in every terminal with a circulation of 150k. I oversee their editorial content, handling all of the big movie interviews. The studios have been awesome to me, and they serve better food than the labels. Also, I've brought Amy along for the ride. I plan on taking over Hollywood.

In addition, on numerous occasions, I've been able to blend my two passions: music and movies. I interviewed the cast of *Twilight,* director Catherine Hardwicke and author Stephanie Meyer about their favorite music. The piece was for Hot Topic's ShockHound.com, and it was one of my favorite pieces that I wrote in 2008. I got Stephanie Meyer, Catherine Hardwicke, the phenomenal Kristen Stewart, Robert Pattinson and Ashley Greene to talk about their favorite music. The piece turned out to be really compelling and revealing, and it's a personal milestone for me, allowing me to bring my two favorite things together. Also, it was great interviewing Ashley Greene. She was extremely cool, and she really dug talking about music. She's another fantastic young talent! I also interviewed *The Uninvited*'s Arielle Kebbel about creating her own soundtrack for *The Uninvited* and that yielded another truly enticing and gripping piece. She's equally awesome! So, everything connects. Music, movies, internships—it all comes full circle.

There will come a time when you need something whether it be a job reference, a good word, or interview, and that little favor that you did will prove to be hugely beneficial. Not to say that the only reason to help people is because they're going to do something for you, being just plain old nice goes a long way. Because I always had a smile on my face while interning at New Line, I made a lot of friends with executives that I wouldn't have necessarily made otherwise. One of those friends led to me breaking into the business through Paul Gargano, former Editor In Chief of *Metal Edge*. People liked me when I started at New Line, and that's what you want. Let the bands put up their middle fingers, and be the badasses. We're not meant to do that. We need as many friends as possible. Still to this day, after I meet someone and get their card, I email them immediately when I get home and say it was nice to meet them. Show that you care. If you say you're going to do something, always do it. That impresses people. So many people in this industry say they're going to do things and then they just don't do them. That leads to mass-disillusionment. When you make good on your promises, it goes an extra long way, because people don't expect that. So when you say you're going to make that call or connection, do it. If things fall through, it's cool because at least you tried. Trying is just as good as making something happen most of the time. The fact that you're willing to give it a shot and that you make good on your promises goes very far and it will lead to much success.

Basically, the most important thing to keep in mind is that each and every thing you do in this industry will have a consequence that shapes your path. Every "break" that we've had has come from a friend in some way. You're always going to need help. So make people want to help you. Show that you're worth they're time, because you are! What better way to do that than to hook them up with something?

Rick Says: I had one contact that wanted an autograph once from his favorite band, so I got it for him. He sent three DVD box sets from the film studio he worked at to thank me. Friends that are there with you from the beginning will be there until the end. Don't forget them. I'll never forget how Amy wrote for the first issue of *Ruin*, or how Paul helped shape me as a writer or how Kristine MSO hooked up all of my first big interviews. Don't forget those people. They will be there after the dust clears, and they'll revel in your success with you.

Amy Says: I concur. Rick and I are enjoying the fruits of a writing partnership where we help each other get gigs and read each other's work. It's that simple. I know if I need another set of eyes on something I've spent an hour on and can't look at it any longer, I can send it to Rick to check out as he does the same for me. We both practice what we are preaching here!

This all sounds simple and very self-explanatory. That's because it is! This goes back to common sense and the golden rule: treat others the way that you want to be treated. There aren't any grades in the music industry. There's no quantitative score on how well you're doing. People don't even care what degree you have at the end of the day. They want to know that they can trust you, rely on you, and that you're going to deliver the goods when it comes down to it. That's what people want. It's not about showing off any statistics. This is an industry based on passion and emotion. Exhibit both of those, be positive and when you can hook someone up, do it. It will come back around and help you at some point. Stay positive, because positivity is infectious. You want people to like you. Let the bands be the bad guys on stage, but know that most of them happen to be the nicest people on the planet in real life. A bad attitude won't get you anywhere in the business world, and at the end of the day, this is the business. Play the game with them, and you're most likely to come away a winner.

Sure, at this point, maybe we sound like a broken record, but the theory is this, and you need to know it, live it, and breathe it. We call it the "More Better Theory:" The more you do, the better you will get. The more you do, the better you will be known. The more you do, the better you will get paid. The more you do, the better your chances are of survival.

IN SUMMATION: If you do for others, they will do for you. It may not always be a quick turnaround, but when you avail yourself, the rest will follow.

BOTTOM LINE:

Do more.

Be better known.

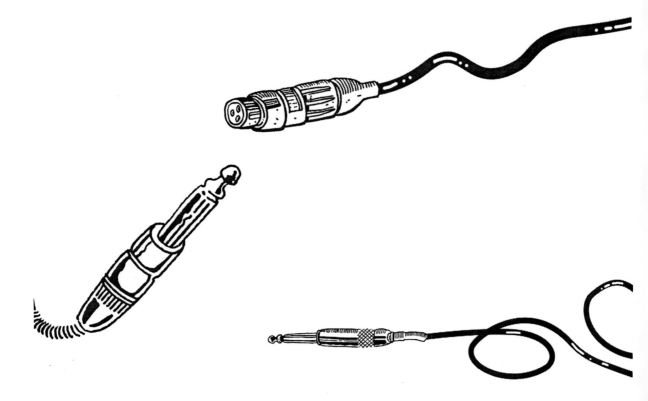

A&R:
If You Are in a Band - TRUST US - You Are Not the Next Big Thing

CHAPTER XIII

This is the most frustrating part of the job. When you are a writer, a publicist, a radio DJ, a promotions person, or an A&R guy, you are constantly hounded by bands who think they are the next big thing. Chances are, they're not. Now if you are in a band and you want to get signed and get exposure, it's good to have and to work local contacts. Play that radio station sponsored "battle of the bands" for a case of beer. Send that press kit and CD to the local entertainment editor at your daily or weekly paper, asking for some ink or some support. Send a promo package to the local radio station for their "local" music specialty show. Make friends with the people who can help you.

But slow your roll. Don't badger, and certainly don't hound them about how you are doing something no one else is doing. Don't think with one demo and one live performance under your belt that you're the next Metallica. You are not ready to perform acoustically at your local radio station. You are not ready to be on the cover of *Rolling Stone* or *Spin* and you are not ready to perform on *SNL*. So don't act like you are. The next big thing happens when a label, which is essentially a money lending institution, like a bank, reaches deep into its pockets and LENDS money to your band. They lend you the money in hopes of making a bigger return on the investment. Remember that when you get signed and go out to dinner and ask the label to pay for your girlfriend's girlfriend at that steak dinner, that's actually coming out of your budget, and you're going to have to recoup on that eventually. Don't be wasteful.

But we're getting ahead of ourselves here. There are many bands out there, and you have to work to get yourself to stand out much like prospective music business people need to make themselves stand out. That requires making a buzz in your local market; give the A&R guy a reason to come see you, to pay for a flight out, a hotel, and a dinner with you.

Some things not to do: do not email someone and ask if you can send them a package, and then write "Solicited Material" on the package. That's annoying enough to make us want to throw the package in the trash without even opening it. If you ask someone if it's okay to send them something, how are they soliciting it from you? Its little things like that that can irritate people with decision-making powers. Do not call incessantly to see if labels/writers/DJs like your music. Try and strike up a personal, real rapport or camaraderie. The music will do the rest of the talking; and your music is, or at least it should be, much more melodious to their ears than the constant sound of your voice nagging and asking for their opinion.

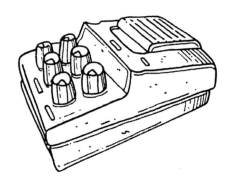

IN SUMMATION: If you are in a band and want to get some recognition using your industry contacts, do it the right way. Don't be "that" guy by being annoying. Do it the right way.

BOTTOM LINE:

Get people to pay attention

By paying attention

Close Encounters of the Metal Kind

CHAPTER XIV

Now, we've both met and interviewed all of our heroes. So we figured we'd include a chapter high-lighting some of the more fruitful, memorable, and downright crazy experiences we've had.

But you've got to remember that when you have the chance to meet band members or people who consider iconic to you, you still have to maintain a modicum of professional decorum. It is no different than conducting yourself like a professional in the office atmosphere when you are interning for a major music business/corporation.

It's okay to ask for autographs, for a photo together, and to recount your biggest fan story. They know you got into this gig in the first place because of your love for them and for music as an art form. But do not—we repeat DO NOT—go overboard. You can't cry, pant, scream, yell, or do a happy dance in front of your interviewee. Don't call your friends and ask the artist to get on the phone with your friend. Don't start crying. That screams "Amateur" at deafening decibels. Sure, you can tell them how much their music has inspired you or how much you love the riff in a particular song, but don't come off as a "fan boy" or "groupie." That'll cause your professionalism to fly out the window and then your subject may not give you the interview that you want for your magazine. Be the pro that we know you are. The playing field is already unbalanced between journalists and rock stars; don't make it even more disparate.

 Amy Says: I've interviewed everyone from Glenn Danzig to Lars Ulrich to Jason New-sted to Stone Gossard to Wendy & Lisa to Papa Roach to Leonardo DiCaprio to Adrien Brody to Leighton Meester to Tom Araya to Pete Wentz to Paula Dorff. Once, I waited three hours for Slash from *Guns 'N' Roses* when he didn't have a proper excuse as to why he made me wait other than "I was doing some stuff" simply because he was fuckin' Slash from fuckin' *G 'N'R*. I've gone dirt track racing and eaten boiled peanuts with a band, engaging in some Southern white trash creature comforts. I've folded Trivium 's laundry with them. I've shadowed Meshuggah on OZZfest for a *Ker-rang!* cover story, where they would break into Swedish when they wanted to say stuff that they didn't want me to hear, and as a journalist, that was understandable.

I've gone drinking in Sweden and Norway with bands because labels flew me out to do interviews. In Flames and Opeth taught me how to curse in Swedish, a tradition that I've taken with me to every OZZfest. I always ask foreign bands on the side stage to teach me how to curse in their native language. Two years ago, Behemoth taught me to cuss in Polish! It always makes for a fun conversation and a little cultural, col-loquial enlightenment. It also breaks the ice, and makes me more comfortable with them and vice versa. I drove Slipknot around in my car on their first OZZFest when they stole stuffed animals out of my car and promptly placed them on their tour bus dashboard. I've gone shopping at a NYC H&M store with Bleeding Through and helped them choose clothing from the retail giant that wasn't in their native Orange County at the time. I sat with Chi Cheng of the Deftones on a boardwalk by the beach in November, talking about

Walt Whitman. I was interviewing Emperor's Ishahn on one line, and had fellow black metal legend, Dani Filth of Cradle Of Filth, leave a message on my other line at the same time!

I had A7X give me a hoodie all the way back when they were opening for Blind Guardian in NYC, before they broke, because they saw me fighting and pouting by their merch table with my "dude" at the time. I had to take Jamey Jasta of Hatebreed to an interview at a radio station in Massachusetts and I drove to his house, parked my car at his crib, and drove his SUV the entire way while he sat in the passenger seat, doing work for his Stillborn label and taking care of business on his Sidekick. I felt like his personal assistant, and I loved it.

So, you name them, I've interviewed them. Probably twice or three times. Most of my high school friends used to gawk and drop their jaws when I would recount tails of who I spent time with and what I did with them while we interviewed, but after 15 years of doing this, it's old hat. I enjoy the art of conversation and engaging in chats with artists, but it's no longer eye-popping to me. I approach it very carefully. I know how I need to act- professional, interested and armed with non-standard questions, including my signature, which is, "Tell me something you don't normally talk about in interviews," which gets them to open up and tell us something about them that isn't written in every other magazine—to get the artist in the zone in order to provide the best, most colorful interview to my editor. That also creates an enlightening piece of positive press on the artist that makes the reader feel like I gave them a sliver of a window of insight into that artist's soul.

You can eventually develop a friendship with the artists you interview or work with, since chances are, you will be supporting them over the course of several album cycles. But remember, that is more often the exception than it is the rule, and many artists do not want to become your best friend simply because you are supporting their work. That is both your job and their job, and it can end after the tape recorder is shut off.

Enjoy the people you do strike up a connection with and don't be worried about those you don't. One band, who shall remain nameless, can thank me for their entire press kit on their second album, but on their fourth album, as a multi-platinum smash,they will not agree to an interview with me. I think it's because I said that I didn't "love" their third album, on which they broke. They even told their publicist that they were worried "Amy is going to trash the record" even after I told them I don't love the new record (at the time) and that I was still going to come to the shows, support them with positive press, and sport their gear proudly. I guess they didn't trust me or believe me when I said that my relationship with them went beyond ONE album in their career. But needless to say, they've refused me interviews since that time. I still go to their shows and give them positive press, because I still love the band, even though their earliest albums were my favorites. That's just part of the game and I don't take it personally.

Make a note: Neither should you. If you take the way an artist treats you as a journalist personally, then you are going to be in for a long, miserable bout of hurt feelings and a heavy load of baggage. Let it go. These people are human beings, not gods.

Sure, I blush and giggle like a school girl when Hatebreed dedicates songs to me on the main stage of OZZfest in front of my entire company and coworkers, or when Dez from DevilDriver screams, "Amy, I love you" in packed, sold out, 3000 capacity crowd in NYC, with all my coworkers and friends there to witness it with me. I also love it when Daryl Palumbo from Glassjaw saw me before a gig in 2002 in Philly and mid-way through the first song, he stopped and sang, "Hi, Amy!" That warms my heart, and makes me happy that I have worked to earn the love and respect of these artists whom I love and respect. They make music that makes my life and my universe a better place, but at the end of the day, it's not why I do it. Maybe this little "Amy Says" is a little self-indulgent, but I work 25/8 and these are the perks that make me love what I do. So many of my friends don't even know what they want to do yet. I am blessed to have figured it out and at such a young age.

That said, there have been times when artists have been dicks to me. I can't express how important it is to maintain your cool in this adversarial moments. Remember that deodorant commercial that said, "Never let them see you sweat!" Heed that advice. Don't let them know that they've razzled you or have gotten under your skin. Play it cool. Keep your cool. Most importantly, do not back down. You are not their prey; you are there to do a service for the band/record, and basic interviews are part and parcel in the promotion of a new album.

When I first met with Lars Ulrich for a chat, I said, "Hi, I'm Amy, I work for *CMJ.*" His reply? "Hi, I'm Lars and I work for James Hetfield." It was a nice, surprising way for him to put me at ease, since you know, he is in the world's biggest rock band. A similar thing happened when I interviewed Stone Gossard of Pearl Jam. He was down to earth to the point of seeming shy, but he was good-natured and answered every question I had, which is a surprise, since a lot of times, publicists will let you know what you can and can't ask in an interview situation.

When I interviewed Glenn Danzig, notorious for his dislike of journalists, at a hotel in Gramercy Park NY, I brought a glossy 8X10 photo for him to sign, and I was a little nervous and said, "I know, I'm a geek." He replied, "You're not a geek." In my nervousness, I said, "No, I know, I really am a geek." He stopped, looked at me and said, "Didn't you hear me? You are not a geek." His tone and the look in his eyes was stern enough to make me shut up, listen, and not say anything else other than questions during the rest of our interview.

Dave Mustaine of Megadeth was another interview that I feared doing. So many journalists said that he wouldn't be an easy or fun interview. He has a reputation for being cagey around writers, but turns out, he and I had a good chemistry. He was personable, affable, and called me by my name the entire time so we were able to enjoy our back and forth. He's one of the most talented metal musicians ever and handling his PR at Roadrunner in 2008 has given me invaluable experience. Same can be said for Slipknot.
My relationship with them is a decade old, starting as writer/supporter and now I have since become their publicist. I have learned so much about managing and handling situations with them that it's made me a better, tougher, more organized publicist who can handle whatever is thrown out. I am grateful, lucky, and proud to call myself their representative.

Henry Rollins is another of my faves. He is famous for challenging journalists, so I was warned to "know my shit" when I interviewed him. I was discussing his benefit album for the West Memphis 3 (the 3 boys in jail for a murder that the evidence proved they didn't commit) so I had to study the facts of the case beforehand.

I called Rollins, who was at the DMV and answered his cell, "Yeah?" immediately launching us into the interview. He was direct, straight up, and informative, and he was intimidating, but never rude. I felt I learned a lot about the case while talking to him by following his lead on the discussions, which is tough for me, being an alpha personality who likes to control conversations.

I've also been given the opportunity to have "all-access" days with certain artists because of my reputation. When I was commissioned by *Kerrang!* to follow Papa Roach around the Anger Management tour with Eminem in Long Island, NY, the band gave me unprecedented access to their tour bus. The singer, Jacoby Shaddix, handed me his CD case and his photo album with pictures of his kids, and said, "Here, take a look." Since it was a piece about being "Inside Papa Roach's life" on a tour headlined by Eminem, the band took things literally and let me inside as though I were a friend. I felt like I was writing an article for *Playboy*, where nothing was kept from me. That was the first time in my life where I felt like a grown-up journalist. I had an "All Access" laminate and Eminem fangirls kept coming up to me and asking me to buy my pass so they could meet Eminem. I politely declined, there was work to do!

My only fan grrrl moment was when I interviewed Philip Anselmo face-to-face. He kept calling me "my love" and every time he did that, I blushed and couldn't hold back the grin. This is Phil Fucking Anselmo, calling me "my love." I have been a fan of his since birth, so to have him speak to me so nicely was a treat. It made me comfortable and I felt like I was talking to an old, forthright friend who also just so happened to be one of my musical heroes.

Another exciting moment in my career was when Slipknot did their first OZZfest, for 2 days in NJ. I somehow ended up driving them around–3 of the 9—since there were so many of them and so much to do, and I was helping the promo reps at Roadrunner out. (Remember, I told you, all the times I helped Roadrunner before I worked there let everyone at the label know who "Amy S" was!) Later that night, Clown and Chris Fehn stole Mr. Potato Head happy meal toys from my car and the next day, backstage at OZZfest, I saw the toys on the dashboard of their tour bus!

I also spent the night hanging out with Joey Jordison outside of a bar, and we traded jackets. I gave him my Hatebreed windbreaker in exchange for his black Adidas zip-up. I still have that hoodie at my house, nearly 10 years later. As I said, today I am one of his publicists and I also worked his side projects and the band he produced, so my relationship with him has grown and morphed over the years and I am constantly enriched by it.

Over the years, I have seen artists yell, kick, scream, and be rude. I have had backstage people comment on why I was running around, chasing down a band. I'd stop and say, "I have a job to do and I'm not here to sleep with anyone. I have a deadline and I need to get paid."

I've also had some of the best, face-to-face conversations of my life. Things I wouldn't trade for the world. Of course, there have been some situations that were bordering on ridiculous. For example, when I was writing for SPIN.com, I was constantly reviewing pop music, like Britney Spears and Sheryl Crow. I had to post my personal email address at the end of each review, for reader feedback, which was fine with me, as it encouraged dialogue with those reading my words. Once, after my review of Britney's debut, I was besieged by emails from her fans, who erroneously thought they had gotten Brit's email address! It lasted for about three weeks and my Yahoo account was deluged with tons of emails. I read most of them, enjoying the innocent nature of her female fans.

Those are just some of the few memories that come off the top of my head. I've been doing this for more than half my life, so it's second nature. My passion hasn't dulled or abetted one bit and for that, I am proud.

I still take interviews with bands that I love or once loved because I want to talk to them about their music, what I love about their music, and how much it means to me.

 Rick Says: I'm still the biggest fan you've ever met. Growing up, I had my drawers labeled by which band t-shirts were housed in them. They were also separated by heavy metal sub-genre. No joke. So, suffice to say, once I met my favorites, I felt fulfilled and truly excited. One of my favorite encounters involved Chad Gray from Mudvayne. I interviewed him at the Long Beach Arena before Mudvayne played to a sold-out crowd with KoRn. I got to the arena 30 minutes before my scheduled interview time, and called the tour manager. He and I met up, and he escorted me through the massive backstage area. We made it to Chad's dressing room and I sat with him while he relaxed with a cup of coffee and Alice In Chains' classic acoustic album *Jar of Flies* playing in the room.

Chad and I talked for 45 minutes. We discussed Jackson Pollock, Pulp Fiction, art, and Mudvayne. It's still one of the best interviews that I've ever done. We delved into the band's music on an intellectual level, and I knew that this article was going to set a standard with Ruin. This was the kind of piece I'd been hoping for. I didn't want to talk about tabloid garbage. Rather, I wanted to go deep inside the music, behind it. Chad was willing, and we connected as artists. He "got it." As I walked out of the dressing room, he called my name "Rick!"

I turned around. "Yeah?"

"Keep working hard, it's going to pay off. I can't wait to see this magazine. Good luck, kid."

"Thank you so much!"

That made my month. I was obsessed with Mudvayne, and here I had just gotten one of my best interviews out of the singer. I called everyone I knew that cared and didn't care to tell them what Chad said.

After that, I had a big interview with another hero, Rob Zombie, while finishing the first *Ruin*. White Zombie was my first favorite "metal" band, and I always really respected Rob as an artist too, because he understood movies and was enmeshed in both arts. Rob's assistant gave me his hotel phone number, a time, and told me to simply ask for "Mr. Black." I usually ate lunch on the 2nd floor patio of New Line (while I was still working in the mailroom), and I would do phone interviews for Ruin or sell ads there on my lunch break. On this specific day, I'd be calling Rob Zombie from there. I sat down in the corner away from the window and dialed. I got the hotel receptionist, asked for "Mr. Black" and was transferred.

Rob picked up immediately, and I planned some amazing questions for him. We talked for about 30 minutes. And as the conversation covered his new record, his films, and growing up in Massachusetts, I noticed he was talkative, but cool, eloquent, and knowledgeable. The interview could not have gone better, and it was going to serve another story mentioned on the cover. He also wished me good luck with the magazine, and emphasized that he wanted to see it once it was out.

My good friends at MSO PR came through and they set me up for a phoner with Jonathan Davis right before KoRn played the Family Values tour with Deftones in L.A. I was so psyched to talk to him and he didn't disappoint. We discussed how music was still cathartic for him and for the fans. We talked about his inspirations and he gave me some great stories about KoRn's early days as well as the storied-Follow the Leader-era. Yet again, I received some positive feedback from the musician about my interview.

I grew up a huge Coal Chamber fan and another amazing Ruin interview was with their singer, Dez, who now fronts the phenomenal band, Devildriver. I talked to Dez Fafara an hour about Devildriver's new record, and he and I just clicked. We instantly became friends through a mutual love of dark books, *Conan the Barbarian*, and Italian food. Dez was just so cool.

He had that vibe of not caring what anyone thought while being charismatic and inspirational. He had been able to reinvent himself in his career—going from Coal Chamber to Devildriver—and still turning people's heads.

Another great interview I did was with Jim Root from Slipknot and Stone Sour. He's one of my favorite guitarists and so we put him on the cover of the third Ruin along with Zakk Wylde and the Trivium axe-slingers. I had hung out with Jim at Family Values, and gave him a copy of *Ruin*. He dug the first magazine and even posted the cover in his guitar case. In the interview, we saw eye-to-eye on a lot of things. I enjoyed delving into art and music. We talked about music from Radiohead to Anthrax, and how to create something that lasts. Jim also discussed playing music for the right reason—because he loved it. At that moment, I realized that I identified more with these musicians who were older than me than I did with people my age. This was what mattered, it wasn't about girls, money or fame. Music was about exploration and providing a perspective in the world.
One of my best interviews for *Ruin* was Joey Jordison of Slipknot . He was impressed when I noticed *Vol. 3* was a concept album, and he mentioned that I was the first person out of all of his interviews to mention that to him . Later, I hung out with him and one of my best friends, Chris "Seven" Antonopoulos [Drummer of Opiate for the Masses, ex-Vanilla Ice], when they were both on the Ministry tour and he remembered me from the interview.

There were three very significant *Ruin* interviews as well. I sat in the KoRn studio talking with Munky until 2am one night. It was a very personal interview. We just sat on the couch in the band's rehearsal space and delved into everything from KoRn's early days, to success, the label, touring, and his views on art. I even had him do a restaurant roundup for *Citysearch.com* of his favorite places to eat. Inside the studio's console room, Munky walked over to a rack of guitars, and picked up a double-necked Gibson. "This one has Jimmy Page's signature on the headstock. It's so cool," he said, while handing it to me for closer inspection. A message from Page to Munky was scrawled on the back, with kind words of encouragement from the master. We sat on that couch for hours, and the talk was amazing.

The second great interview in that same month involved Dino from Fear Factory which happened while enjoying Mexican food and talking about his new bands. In Hollywood, there's a popular Mexican Restaurant, called El Compadre, on Sunset Boulevard across from the original Guitar Center. They featured a nightly Mariachi band, gigantic margaritas, and traditional enchiladas. It's here that *Ruin* met with ex-Fear Factory / Brujeria guitarist and current Asesino axe-slinger Dino Cazares. He was seemingly dormant since ties were severed with Fear Factory in 2002, but as he describes it—with both Asesino and Divine Heresy—he's "back with a vengeance." As vengeful as the gold-selling guitar god may be, we still had to wait 30 minutes for a table. Cazares, being the charmer he was, walked up to a server and quickly asked something in Spanish. After winning a response, he replied "Dos" with both fingers. Unfortunately, the suave request lead to nothing more than another 30 minutes of waiting, but … we eventually got our enchiladas and delved into Cazares' two current projects, offering *Ruin* an exclusive look at the soul of this new machine.

Then, there was the day I got held hostage by Zakk Wylde. This was that story: Zakk Wylde's "Compound" sits on top of a Southern California mountain with no cell phone reception and a lone dirt road leading to it. On this particularly rainy Saturday, the road was especially fun to drive as cars nearly fish tailed off and into oblivion at each winding curve. It's also very easy to get lost up there in the vacant darkness, which was exactly why the Ozzy Osbourne guitarist and Black Label Society main man liked it.

Later on that day, while sitting in his favorite local bar, Wylde went up to the jukebox and selected Patsy Cline's "Crazy" for the fifth consecutive time. Then he sat back down and loudly reiterated for us, "Black Label Society are the motherfucking kings of the jungle. The remote, "wild" location of his home backed that notion up 100 percent. Once we reached the top of the mountain, the house commanded all attention, with a circular driveway, homemade half pipe, basketball hoop, large pool, and back house. The garage doors were wide open, and Wylde sat lifting weights as my photographer and I pulled up. This garage was something of a sanctuary for him. Posters of his heroes covered the walls. Magazine cut-outs of Randy Rhoads, Eddie Van Halen, Jimi Hendrix, Ozzy, and Jimmy Page adorned almost every inch of space. The rest was plastered with street signs for Thurman Munson and Babe Ruth, and numerous pictures from Maxim, FHM, and Stuff.

Clad in a cut-off denim shirt, the jacked six-foot rocker might be mistaken for the most intimidating 14-year-old guitar prodigy ever. However, being the benevolent host he was, the second we walked in, we were greeted with two cold beers and a bear hug of death. He immediately began a tour of the house, taking us into a tiny room filled with his favorite guitars, memorabilia, gifts from friends like the late Dimebag Darrell, and most impressively, a vest worn onstage by the legendary Randy Rhoads.

Before we got started with the interview, the legend demanded five reps with a 130 lb barbell from me. Somehow, those reps got done, and Zakk smiled, "That's fucking Black Label brother!" slapping me on the back with a pronounced thud and I felt my spine cracking.

"Onto leg exercises," he yelled. First, he requested that we all don the Mexican wrestling masks he just bought to ensure what he calls "pure comedy." I couldn't see through the Mexican mask and my jeans got caught on the machine. After I tripped, fell, jabbed my hip on the bench's edge and smacked my head on a hanging barbell, Wylde screamed "Black Label down!" and he hoisted me up into a head lock. Finally, after two hours of beer and calisthenics … we got to the interview. He handed me another beer and we began talking about his heroes, his dreams, what "Black Label" means and why Black Label Society will one day take over the world. That was absolutely insane.

Another huge interview for me was with Corey Taylor of Slipknot and Stone Sour. I talked to Corey about comic books and movies in his dressing room before Stone Sour played the House of Blues in Anaheim. The second I walked in the dressing room, I could tell he was tired, but I had something fun planned. Instead of asking the same questions that he's heard a million times about Stone Sour, Slipknot, and the road, we talked about what inspireed him for about an hour. It was one of the best interviews I'd ever done and one of the last I'd conducted for Ruin. We talked for about an hour. It showed me how to talk to artists outside of the box.

Once I got my gig at ARTISTdirect, I became blessed with the chance to do anything. I started hooking up interviews constantly. I got other DREAM interviews for the web site: Snoop Dogg, Phil Anselmo of Pantera and Down, Wes Borland, Vinnie Paul, and Chad Gray, and then the biggest and best, Slash. I'd idolized a lot of these people growing up so this was really gratifying for me to have the opportunity to interview them.

Continuing along the lines of our message that working in this industry is about commitment and lifestyle, I've also helped the artists with writing, once I had a relationship with them. I've done all of the bios for Emotional Syphon Recordings [Munky of KoRn's label] because they respected and trusted me. Chino Moreno [Deftones & Team Sleep Frontman] remains one of the most amazing people I've ever met. His commitment to true art still inspires me today. I worked with Chino on the launch of his Skater Socks company, ChinoSox, by writing his bio, building his web site and MySpace, and helping with publicity and marketing because he's got an immense amount of artistic integrity—always choosing to be true to himself above all. Every word that he records bleeds passion and emotion. He's also one of the most genuine and down-to-earth people that I've ever met. I'm honored to call him a friend, and I'll always think he's the best vocalist ever. Working with him and interviewing him has been one of the best experiences of my time in the music business, not to mention that he's got great taste in movies, music, books and art! I have also worked closely with his girlfriend Risa Mora, who in addition to being awesome in every way, is a hell of a cook!

These are examples of how to handle yourself and how to do it right. If you're a hipster or an elitist but you take on that story with a more mainstream band because you need the money, do not walk into that interview with the attitude that you are holier than thou and display zero respect for the artist or their music. You're not that important and neither is your opinion. Be a rock journalist, not a rock critic. Everyone hates (but has to deal with) those Ivory Tower residing rock journalist dinosaurs who won't leave their posts till they die, so don't follow their lead; let them die out. If you are a journalist, you are covering a scene, a beat. If you are a critic, you are making judgments and if you can't play those songs to scale on your OWN guitar, then you better just watch what you say.

Don't take yourself too seriously. Remember this is rock 'n' roll and if you can't have fun in rock 'n' roll, then you are in the wrong business. You don't have to go get drunk every happy hour because you hate your life and your job when you are living and working in the rock 'n roll universe. Start having a pulse and vibrancy.

IN SUMMATION: Make friends with the bands – When you have the opportunity, show them your work and build a name for yourself. It is CRUCIAL to let them know you are working for them, because they will repay the favor. Sure, you may not get paid TODAY for the feature or review you wrote, or that time you played their record on the college radio station you worked at, but remember, when the band becomes huge, you were there first. And you can use that as your OWN calling card.

BOTTOM LINE:

If you can make friends with bands, good.

If not, still good.

Conduct yourself professionally at all times.

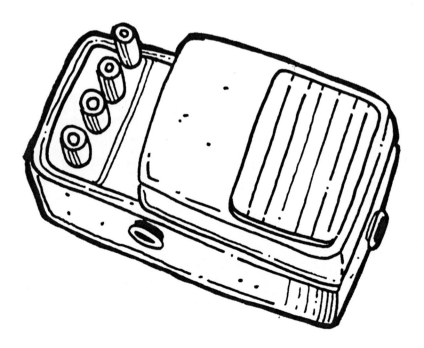

It's Not Just a Job; It's a Lifestyle and an Adventure

CHAPTER XV

Now that we've said most of the important stuff, it's time to send you off into the music business sunset, but not before we outfit you with one final piece of advice that you need to heed and fully comprehend now or you will never survive amongst the wolves and coyotes. The music business is not just a job. It's not even a career. It's a way of life. It's a lifestyle. It's an adventure. When you decide to embark on a career in this industry, you need to accept and know full well going into it that you are giving up your nights, weekends, and free time in order to make it. Once you put in a few good hard years of indentured servitude, then you can make more time for fun, hobbies, relationships, and kids. But for now, your job is your life. But hey, it's not so bad. It's not like you are going to jail or are going to work a corporate job that sucks out your soul and makes you forget that you're a human being. Think of all your friends from college who have to escape to a bar for happy hour after working a 9-5 day at the job they hate. You will love your job; you will love your lifestyle. You will be the envy of all your friends, who want to know, "Hey, dude, how can I get a cool job like you!" If we had a nickel for every time one of our non-music business friends said that very statement to us, we wouldn't be scribbling this tome; we'd be sunning our fine bodies on some sandy white beach next to a warm, crystal-clear, shark-free body of water in a tropical location where everyone's happy and smiling. Remember that scene in *Little Miss Sunshine* when the formerly mute brother says, "Love what you do; fuck the rest." No truer words were ever spoken. Not to get all Velveeta on your ass, but when you love what you do, you're alive. Spending 8 hours a day waiting for the end of the work day to get here so you can stop doing what you hate has to suck! We would never want to live like that, and neither should you.

But above all, if anything, navigating the murky music business waters will prepare you for future endeavors or whatever path you chose to go post-music business or even how far up the ladder you want to climb. You will be prepared for whatever shit life throws at you. Once you've put in a few years and paid dues in the music industry, everything else is just cake and a cakewalk.

Good, now that you have accepted this fact of music business life, you can set about the task of succeeding and becoming the music business tastemaker, high stakes player, mover and shaker that you always wanted to be. Knowing this and accepting this from the outset will prevent any shock or anger when you realize you have to work all weekend, even if it's not at your desk. Remember GI Joe? "Knowing is half the battle." So now you know. You are already half way to the finish line, friend!

When we say that it's not just a job or a career but a lifestyle, we mean that it's a lifestyle. Prepare for long hours. If you are East Coast based, then prepare to stick around till 8 or 9 PM so that you are synched up with the West Coast faction of the business. The business day doesn't stop just because it's 6 PM on the East Coast. Expect Friday night phone calls if you are dealing with artists. Expect 3 AM phone calls on Sundays when an artist has missed his or her flight and needs your help in rebooking them, pronto. Expect a temperamental artist having a hissy fit because he or she is unhappy about the way the marketing plan on the record is going. They'll expect you to be their shrink for an hour. Prepare to be a sounding board, a shrink, and to have no one listen to you when you think you have a great idea. Nevermind that you want to stack Zs or catch up on your much lost beauty sleep. You are always on call, like a doctor, but without the golf-game-on-days-off salary.

Speaking of doctors, you are not one. This is not life saving work nor is it rocket science, but it is life enhancing. For you, for the artists you are working with, and for the people who are exposed to the artist through whatever task you have done to expose the artist. You are working for the good and promotion of art, something that gets us all through those shitty days, so don't ever let someone tell you that what you are doing is useless, small scale, or not a real job. Whoever says that is just jealous and hates that he or she has to suck up to the man day in and day out and secretly wishes deep down that they had your job and your talent and skill. So remember, and this is imperative, to enjoy the cool job you have. It is true that the music business has a near 100% turnover rate, with plenty of people with truckloads of experience throwing in the towel, throwing up their hands and moving on to do something more lucrative or life-changing after many years of toiling. That doesn't have to be you. Learn to pace yourself and make "I am lucky to have such a cool job" your mantra, on constant rotation on a repeat loop in your skull. Know it. Live it. Love it. You'll thank us later.

Your weekends will consist of answering emails on your handheld device. It will consist of attending concerts or catching up on emails from the week that you couldn't get to because you were too busy dealing with something else. You will have to do interviews on the weekends. You will have some sort of business that needs immediate attending to on your "off hours." There are no off hours, especially if you start out as an assistant. You should, by the way, always get to work before your boss and never leave work before your boss if you are just starting out and are an assistant. Make sure his or her needs are super served and served above your own. Don't be the last one in and the first one to go. You are probably going to start out at the age of 22 or so, so you probably won't have kids or any other deep commitments. If you do have other commitments in your life that you can't split your attention and time with, then you definitely need to rethink what you are getting into, what your significant other can handle, and what your ultimate life goals are anyway!

Late hours. Long days. Weekends filled with work. No life. Not a lot of sleep. You might be scratching your head and second guessing why the hell you want to be involved in this crazy business when you have to make such sacrifices, especially in the beginning stages of your career. But all you have to do is pull out your favorite album of all time, take a listen, and remember how good it felt to fall in love with that band or that particular song, or whatever sparked that desire within you to be a part of something special.

When you are part of a band breaking – whether you are a journalist, a publicist, the first DJ to play the band on commercial radio airwaves or the first agent to book them live, whatever- you will sprint to your desk every day to see what else the press is saying, how many units were moved, how many pre-sale tickets were sold for the upcoming tour, and how the bloggers are reacting to said band. It's a wonderful, breath-taking, nearly orgasmic feeling to be a part of an organic thing like breaking a band.

Music saves lives. Getting music to the right ears or the ears that just need to hear it is one of the most rewarding things you can ever be a part of. You can be cocky for a moment and pat your own damn self on the back and say, "Shit, I did that. I had something to do with that" when a band sells a million copies of a record. That feeling is what drives us all in this crazy business.

There you have it. All the things you need to break into the music business and how to survive the current crisis of shrinking CD sales. Look out for you and watch your own back, and you will be golden no matter what you do in life.

Just remember this one final adage: no music, no life. Recorded music is precious. Once the business model rebounds and the record industry rebuilds and reforms its systems, you will be malleable, bendable, and flexible, and ready to change with the times because you are equipped with the know-how and the ambition to do so.

Good luck. We hope to cross paths with you many times during your successful career.

Love,

Amy & Rick

PUT THIS BOOK DOWN AND MAKE SOMETHING HAPPEN NOW

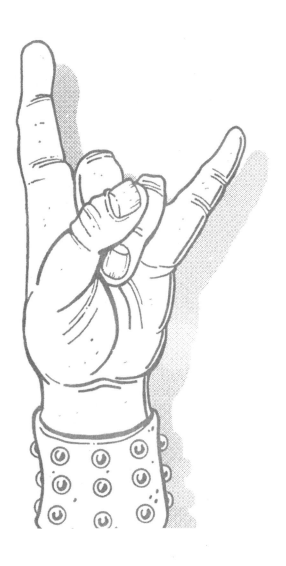

From Rick:

I'm really lucky to have worked with some phenomenal people at the studios and movie publicity firms. Even though I've only been writing about movies since 2007, everyone in the film business has been incredible to me! (That's not to say the music people haven't because they rule too, but I've been at that since 2004!) Some of those extraordinary movie folks include: Tamar Teifeld, Casey Stone and Kyle Bonnici and everyone at Paramount, Samantha Kolker and everyone at Paramount Vantage, Tamara Trione and Leah Vail Soloff and everyone at Nancy Seltzer & Associates, Kate Hubin, Jamie Blois and everyone at Lions Gate, Orna Pickens, Gemma Cacho and everyone at Warner Bros., Mac McLean and everyone at Click Communications, Nicole Canizales, Ryan Fons, Mike Rau, Mike Liotta—also, everyone else that I've worked with at Disney, Universal, Warner Bros., Paramount, Sony, Fox, Disney, BWR, PMK, 42 West and so on and so forth.

(Lastly, because I can't help it, a few more shout outs to some friends who have been integral on my personal journey—Cheryl Feiz (My mother whose inspired every good thing I've done, I love you more than I can ever truly express), Richard J. Florino Jr. a.k.a. "Big Rich" (My dad and the reason I got into movies and music. He's the coolest guy ever, and the best dad anyone could ever ask for), Amy Sciarretto (Wouldn't be here without you!), Dave Delaney (My best friend from high school!), Tony Caso (The man who introduced me to Pantera and my longest friend), my brother Pat McCarron (I'll never forget all those great times and great shows, thanks you for always being there), Paul Gargano ('nuff said, I would not be here without you), James Patrick, Janet Florino, Siobhan McCarron, Liz McCarron, Drew "Vagina Man" Fin-Kelson (My screenwriting partner-in-crime, an immense positive influence and an amazing dude), Corey Soria (Watch out, he's going to break some ground with the camera, he's also just an incredible person!) Hyro da Hero (You are the resurrection and future of hip hop!), Rika O'Connor (Best Director of Communications Ever and the big sister I never had), Chino Moreno (I can't even begin to express how much of an inspiration you are), Risa Mora (Only person that can cook better than I can), Lola, Kobe, Kristian, Benjie Gold (Thank you for everything, you're going to be on top where you belong!), Kevin Estrada (The nicest and most talented photographer ever), Ken Blaustein (A true music sage, and a hell of a friend), Andrew Bennett (My favorite music video director, another true talent!) Dominique Swain (You're an amazing actress and person!), Andrew Gargano, Danny Ornelas, Eric German, George Vallee, Frank Gatto, Doug Simpson, Mike Moses (Thanks for everything!), Kim Estlund (Finally, someone that loves *Twilight* as much as me in the music biz! Thank you for everything! You're amazing), Natalie Geday (Another partner-in-my-plan for global domination), David "Beno" Benveniste (You're a true inspiration!), Mark Wakefield, Gus Canazio, Graham Martin and everyone at Velvet Hammer, Mitch Schneider, Kristine Ashton-Magnuson, Libby Henry and everyone at MSO, Gary Richards, Tom Davidson, James "Munky" Shaffer and all of KoRn, Paul Gray, Joey Jordison, Jim Root, Corey Taylor and all of Slipknot, Christy Priske, Rick Canny, Raymond Herrera, Christian Olde Wolbers, Ben Bledsoe, Aaron Lewis and all of Staind, Chad Gray and all of Mudvayne, Dez Fafara, Jeff Kendrick, John Boecklin, Jon Miller and Mike Spreitzer of Devildriver, Dave Navarro and all of Camp Freddy, Team Sleep, Deftones, Ryan DeMarti (We need to hit more Down, Gwar and Metallica shows!), Wayne Static and all of Static-X, Zakk Wylde, Shavo Odadjian, RZA, Baby Bash, Ed Ocañas, Frankie J, Matt Sorum and all of Velvet Revolver, Ashley White, Christina Kotsamanidis, Jillian Marie Giblin and all at Atlantic Records, Max Noce, Chris Stankee, Dallas Coyle, Doc Coyle and all of God Forbid, Tom Capone, Kelli Scott, Kerli, Paul Freeman, Aoife and all of Moth Complex, Dino Cazares, J-Dog, Johnny 3 Tears, Charlie Scene, Da Kurlzz, Deuce and Funny Man of Hollywood Undead, Joby Ford and all of The Bronx, Troy Sanders and all of Mastodon, Tim Williams and all of Bloodsimple, Jacoby Shaddix, Tobin Esperance, Jerry Horton and Tony Palermo of Papa

Roach, Black Tide, Jimmy Sullivan and all of Avenged Sevenfold, Max Cavalera and all of Soulfly, Robb Flynn and all of Machine Head, Kevin Chiaramonte and everyone at Universal Republic, Renee Harrison and everyone at Interscope, Rome Thomas, Val Pensa and everyone at A&M/Octone, Rick Gershon, Brian Bumbery and everyone at Warner Bros., Kristen Mulderig, Nick John and all at The RSE Group, Karen Wiessen and Aishah White at Island/Def Jam, Fernando Aguilar, Chase Polan, Jamie Roberts, Kim Bowen, Bob Bowen, Paul Broucek, Matt Leos, Lindsay Harrington, Robert "Nick" Nicholson, Jonathan Cohen and everyone at Zen Media Group, Jessica Ricci and everyone at Roadrunner Records, Cory Brennan, Seven Antonopoulos, Anna Kjellberg, George Borkowski, Kim Swartz, Jamie Teissere and all of Droid, Mandi Arvizu, Shannon Crawford, Bill Yetz (I can't even express my thanks for everything, you're a foundation of positivity in my life), Nana Barbara and Papa Clem, Shirley and Joe, Donna and Holly, Kim and Pat, Kenny and Anna, Bobby and Wendy, Ronnie and Marybeth, Grandma, Auntie Joanie, Darlene and Ken, Nicole Paxson (We've had some adventures, there are only more to come!), Siobhan Higgins and all at *LAX* Magazine, Michael Potts, Chas Reynolds, Heidi Atwal, Jay Watford, Francis Zapanta and everyone at ARTISTdirect.com, Robert Moritz, Jay Herrati, Rob Angel, Mar Yvette and everyone at Citysearch.com, Dan Epstein, Randy Bookasta and everyone at Shockhound.com—the rest of my friends and family and finally and anyone and everyone that I've ever worked with in any capacity in this crazy world of show business, THANK YOU!!!)

The Last two interviews I need to do for music—Eminem and Scott Weiland. That's all that's left on my idols list for music! Movies, that's another story, maybe another book!!!! I love movies more than anything! They're my lifeblood! I have my Dad, Scorsese, Hitchcock, Ford, Eastwood, Kubrick, Coppola and countless others to thank for that!

Watch out for my upcoming books *Ruined*, *Dolor* and my screenplay, *I.L.V*, VERY SOON!!! Plus, there's even more stuff I'm working on now, while you're reading this…

Thanks from Amy Maria Sciarretto:

The Fam: Dad (PW), Mom (Chez), Johnny, Marlie, Phil, Jolene, Courtney, Paige, Aaron, Anthony and my pets that I miss a ton: Puffy, Rascal, Fiarella, Brandon.

The Extended Fam: Mike Zara (OHD, Mmmmmmm), Brad Filicky (old and gray), Mike Smith (BFN!), Rennie Resmini, Rick Florino (partners in crime!), Maddie and Chris Smith, Renee Crowley (NSB!), Mike Gitter, Laurie and Bob Wolfe, Taeko Saito, Amy Tso, Aimee and Eric Millard, Sam Lennon (MAC!), Jamey Jasta, Bram Tietelman (my first boss, South Jersey for life), Ron Platzer (a major shaper of my career's formative years), Jason Rudolph (1997, at a South Jersey hotel in NJ, "Amy, you could totally write for the trades!"), Dave Ciancio (LBS, CoasterMission '00), Eric Peltier, Eric Cole, Tara Buzzell, Marc Meltzer, Ben Markese, Mat Pileggi, Brian Rocha, Ed Martin, Jose and Melissa Mangin, Eddie and Dez (for insisting I be at the '07 record release party), the Roadrunner family, Cees Wessels, Jonas Nachsin, Dave Loncao, Elias Chios, Mark Abramson, Jessica Ricci, Madelyn Scarpulla, Nelson Mitchell, Rich Perkins, Rose Slanic, DeanPogue, Michael Canter, Kathie Merritt, Harlan Frey, Justin D'Angelo, Thom Scarzynski, Austin Stephens, Renee Duncan, Karen Dillett, Monte Conner, Dave Rath, Phil Kaso, Laura Bender, Jason Martin, Billy Cox, Ron Burman, Suzi Akyuz, Chris Brown, Jeff Kish, Angela "Relli" Gnagnarelli (Treatage), Steve Bresalier, Jon Satterly, Ray Garcia, Sharanda Houser, Chakeesha McCalla, Yarrow Banerjee, Andrew Carpenter, Mike Easterlin, Jeremy Rosen, Lauren Kufta, Kathi Sheasby, Joan Bolvin, Sarah McKenzie, Tara Frank, Jasper Schuurmanns, Michelle Kerr, Kirsten Lane, Sami Westwood, Danielle Samerhoff, Steve Artz, Veronica Vallado and Carl Schultz, Marc Schapiro, Matt Polen, Dan Forman, Maria Gonzales, Jamie Roberts, Kevin Estrada, Rob Weldon, Ally Hearne, Kevin Boyce, Mike Boyle, Joe Wrenn, Ryan Adams (Amilou), Kristen Anderson, Mark Nunez, Colin Frangicetto, Aub Driver, Patty Pelle, Sarah Beck, Megan White, Julie Vecchio, Chris Torres, Maria Ferrero, Dana Bove, Terri Craft, Eric Kaplan and Joe Kirschen, Bobby Haber, Glen Sansone, Cheryl Botchick, Colin Helms, Alex Ellerson, Scott Frampton, Jordan Mamone, Bill Werde, Moose, Kory Grow, Jon Rayvid, Tom Beaujour, Barb Rubenstein, Brad Tolinski, Jason Pettigrew, Aaron Burgess, Andy Secher, Mitch Hershkowitz, Seth Werkheiser, Albert Mudrian, Andy Gensler, Ron Hart, Jeff Kitts, Andrew Apanov, Ilko Nechev, Siobhan Higgins, Jessica Miller, Cara Schultz, Kimberly McDonald, Candice Sabatini, Dina Fierro, Octavia Laird and Rodney, Roberto Hernandez, Jessica Siracusa, Joe Molinaro, Ryan Graden, Jen Meola, Cory Brennan, Mike Boyle, Irene Richter, Anne Kristoff, Gus Pena, Jeff "Met" Thies, Paul Barretta, Liz Ciavarella, JJ Kocz,an, Dave Everly, Dan Brown, Brian Bumbery, Heidi Atwal, Vaughn Lewis, Kenny Gabor, Justin Arcangle, Steve McTaggart, John Bambino, Alisha Turull, Dave Vagasky, Loana dP Valencia, Kathi Haruch, Heath Miller, Scott Lynch and Stacy, George Vallee, Karen Wiessen, Kelli Malella, Jerry Graham, Tom Wojcik, Heather West, Libby and Kristine at MSO, the Doc, Eric Brocki, Mike Cubillos, Meg Young, Mike Ski, Rosa my colorist, Sarah my stylist, LeAnne Kohlbecker, every band I've worked with at Roadrunner, every movie and music publicist and every beauty publicist I have ever worked with! There are too many of you to name, but if I forgot you, all you have to do is email me and you'll get a personal thank you from me. All of you have helped in my goal of being able to turn what I love –music, writing about music and promoting music- into a sustained, successful career! Here's to getting an article in *Vanity Fair* one day!

APPENDIX

We asked some of our favorite musicians and closest friends about the future of the music industry.

Here's what they had to say...

Chino Moreno
Vocals & Guitar
Deftones // Team Sleep

How has the music business changed since you started your career? What's your opinion on the changes?

A lot has changed in this business since I started my career in 1994. One of the more notable things I've realized that has changed is the concept of "Artist Development." My band was lucky enough to have a label that was interested in helping us build and develop our brand. They also gave us time to grow as a band as opposed to just putting our record out and seeing if it would stick or not.

What advice would you give to young aspiring industry-types? What qualities did you find comforting in writers, label people, publicists, etc?

Find people, bands, artists, etc. that you are actually into and that you can see yourself being involved with for the long haul. Also know that it's very rare that things just happen overnight. Be patient and stay dedicated.

Where do you see the music industry going?

Sadly I don't see anything getting better until people are ready to take chances and start putting their heads out a little more. A lot of the old ways are quickly changing due to technology and I think it should be embraced instead of run from.

Is being a fan more important than anything else?

Not necessarily, but it is important to enjoy what you do and who you choose to work with. Being passionate about your work will only make you and those you associate with work harder and be even more dedicated.

James "Munky" Shaffer
Guitar - KoЯn
Vocals & Guitar - Fear and the Nervous System
Founder/CEO - Emotional Syphon Recordings

How has the music business changed since you started your career? What's your opinion on the changes?

There's been a shift in the business. I felt that before I started my label—Emotional Syphon Recordings. I had a vision of doing an artist-run label-as I'm an artist, and I like to keep working. Plus, there's always work if you want there to be work. You go get it; it's not going to come to you-like you know. So I felt the shift subconsciously that the business was going to change, and I didn't know if it was going to be the right time to start a label, but I feel like it was, by coincidence maybe. It's just another example that if you follow what you believe in, it will come true. I wanted to do something, because the industry's been crooked. With the corporations, if it was done the right way then we wouldn't have so many people without jobs. With the downloading though, the curve wasn't set up right, and the technology got ahead of the industry. I wanted to do something that catered to artists. There are so many good musicians out there. With my band KoЯn, I was lucky to make that cut before the end of an era, thank God. I'm grateful for the fact that my family lives a good life because of all my hard work. So I want to pay my success back with this label. I also want to hopefully create something that's fair between artist and label because we need each other. I call people on the phone myself. I like to meet them. We do exchange emails, a lot. But I have personal contact with everyone that's in the family because that's how a label should be run: face to face and with a handshake. Let's be gangsters here [laughs]. No, I'm just kidding. We don't have to do that because we make our money and product honestly as artists. Everybody knows that, especially artists. There are misconceptions in the business that artists just sit with their feet up all day. Well if I had time to do that, I wouldn't because I'd be busy making music [laughs]. Even with the downloading and the big labels collapsing, there are still opportunities to have a career in this industry. So the changes haven't necessarily made things bad. Things are just different.

What advice would you give to young aspiring industry-types? What qualities did you find comforting in writers, label people, publicists, etc?

Be passionate first and foremost. Passion is what drives music. If you're passionate, working with artists is a lot easier. Never give up either. It's not an easy business, but it's worth it. We need to just concentrate on making great art.

Where do you see the music industry going?

I think the music is going back into the artist's hands, which is the right place for it. The fans always rule at the end of the day, and once the major labels all disappear, the fans and bands will still be there.

Is being a fan more important than anything else?

Yes, I would say so. None of us would be here if we weren't fans. You have to love what you do in order to truly do it well, and that couldn't be truer for music.

Shavo Odadjian
Bass – System of a Down
Bass/Composer/MC/Producer – Achozen
Founder – urSESSION.com

How has the music business changed since you started your career? What's your opinion on the changes?

When I started with System of a Down, the Internet wasn't so in control of music. It didn't guide the careers of artists, and on the other end, the careers of sellouts. There are the artists, and then there are the people that do it for money and only for money. They replicate what's already been done. They make money off it. Then they drop out, buy their houses in Fiji, and they're done. The Internet has shaped the form of the music industry. When System was shopping for labels, there were like six or seven labels out there in '96 and '97. Now there are what, three? Those three are suffering and struggling to stay afloat. They're buying each other out like whores with pimps. The pimps are the fucking chairmen of the board. That's what's going down. Our music is getting pimped, and our babies are becoming whores. So I'd rather release music for free, hopefully in the future. That comes in with my site urSESSION.com. urSESSION came from a brainstorm between me and my friend Narb, who has been my best friend since first grade. I was trying to figure out how to discover new artists. We've got this artist named Leggezin Fin. He's from Angola, Africa. I was like, "Damn, this motherfucker's amazing." If someone hadn't found him and brought him to America as a foreign exchange student in art school, and we hadn't gotten the opportunity to put him on tracks like the Achozen stuff. The fact that we found some dude from Angola whose talented far beyond most of the artists out there making loot right now who are in the limelight made me think, "How do we find more artists that are in that world?" These artists are so good but they come from places where they may not have the ways to record their demos or they have no means to have that demo be heard by someone. Their uncle is not someone connected at a label. So I thought of a way to create a music community online—like an online art district where it's by artists for artists. So it's beneficial for artists, and I'm putting myself outside of that fish bowl right now because I did create the site, and it is a business venture. Take out all the bullshit, and it's a venture of finding artists. It's a hunt. It's more like a crusade. Let me be the one that holds the torch and runs. You find artists like Kinetic-9 and Rev. William Burke or Chameleon Conductor and Snot. Those are bands and artists that have "it." "It" meaning the ability to perform, the ability to write, the ability to create, but don't conform to what is being done in the industry as we speak. How do we get these artists to be heard, seen and respect? That's what they deserve: respect. I.E. System of a Down in 1997, the person that became our A&R guy was the same person telling us to change singers prior to Rick Rubin finding us. That's where we run. That's where I'm trying to get the world to revolve around artists and not around the people that shape the lives of artists—the industry people. How did GZA put it, "Who's you're A&R—a mountain climber who plays the electric guitar?" Come on now, that's so frickin' true, honest and real. It's real today.

What advice would you give to young aspiring industry-types? What qualities did you find comforting in writers, label people, publicists, etc?

One word, commitment, is a common denominator. The artists share that with everyone in the industry. Belief is a part of it, and both commitment and belief go hand-in-hand in what you're doing. It's easier to say that than to be a part of it because the industry today is like a snake pit. Once you fall in, you either have to be a snake charmer or get bitten and killed. A snake charmer is a bullshitter because he bullshits the snake to make him believe that everything is all good until he does what he does, takes the snake and makes it charmer-friendly by taking out the venom. He takes out the most beautiful, natural thing that the snake had—that venom, that ability to strike. The snake charmer takes that away from him and makes him into a limp little long reptile that doesn't have that ability. That's what a label does to an artist. It takes away the integrity. It takes away the fangs, the venom that the artist would've had if he or she wasn't led by the industry. If you want to be a writer, take it from Rick Florino. Individuality matters. I could speak about each position one by one. If you're a striving writer, you're an artist, man. A writer is an artist. Think before you write. Don't write what's been written. Don't follow what's been done. Find your own little avenue, take it and believe in it. Don't just find an avenue, not believe in it and think, "Oh, this is different." No, you've got to believe in what you're doing, follow it and do it. Go! They say divine minds bond. They unify as one. A divine is not only someone that can preach you divine words but someone that can also write down divine words about a divine artist who speaks about divine things. Recognize each other. Don't change. Don't conform. The artists, people and individuals who conform stifle the cause. The cause is originality and integrity. It's motherfuckers that think, "Oh, I tried this for a year and a half or two years and it didn't work so now I'm going to do what everyone else is doing and sell my ass." Well, you're the one that is halting the movement. Stick with it for three years, four years, and five years. If you don't make it, at least you stood your ground. At least you did what you believed in and didn't do what was proven successful ten years ago. What about ten years from now?

Don't look at ten years ago, look at ten years from now. Look at the present, think of the future, and don't look at the past because the past has been done.

Yes, the past can be re-done. But it's just like recycled water. You don't wash your dishes with someone else's backwash, do you? Will they be clean?

Where do you see the music industry going?

That's a fucking really good question, Rick. I personally can't give you a straight answer on that one. I'd love to, but right now we're at a place in not just the music industry but in business and money where we've gone through this whole recession. There's going to be a change in leadership within the strongest power of the world. The world's about to have a new chief. Just like recycled music, you want recycled leaders. What's proven to be good—the 85 percenters are happy with that. They're down to have the same thing as long as they go to their nine-to-fives, as long as they drive their Prius's, as long as they get to watch *As the World Turns* on *Tivo* when they get home from work. They're happy with that. They're afraid of change. Most of the world is afraid of change, so I don't know where it's headed. The Internet is where it's at. By the time this hits print, if there are three now, there may be two or one label left. You never know. Unless they conform and adapt to what's going on, I think independent labels, independent companies and independent ideas are the future. Those independent ideas, independent labels, independent companies and independent thoughts need independent backing and independent listeners. There is a game out there called monopoly, and I think that's the way of America. What if there is something out there that's as good as the classic records I grew up on that changed the cycle? How do you know that record hasn't already been recorded somewhere in Wichita, Kansas or Lithuania and you're just never going to hear it. There is just so much out there. That's why I did urSESSION. What I'm seeing through urSession, the ones that are getting the most votes are the ones that I would predict that 85 percenters would vote for so what I do is what I go on there, I don't check who got the most votes, I go right down the middle, not who got the least, but who got the middle amount. Those are the artists that aren't ready made. When you go to McDonalds and you order a Big Mac, if you don't say, "No onions" that shit's coming right off the conveyor belt, and it was probably cooked an hour ago. You have to change it a little bit to have it cooked brand new for you so you can have it warm, new and flavorful. That's a great analogy also. In music, art and life, switch things around. As a writer, as a reporter, as someone in the industry, as whatever you are, flip the fucking script on the motherfuckers. You might not be heard or respected the first or second time, but the third or fourth time, people have to listen and people have to convert. If something's good, it's good. Anything really good isn't recognized the first time around. Some people never get it, but at least they're there and they exist and they give others the opportunity to be heard. They give inspiration. Hearing a band like Muse be so famous and big gives me hope. I'm enlightened and happy that at least there's some fucking hope that there are some good bands out there. That's the biggest band right now that I think is doing shit for the right reasons. They're keeping it flat. They're waving the flag of their fathers—their fathers being who they are inspired by and guided by. Your fathers are your mentors and inspirations.

Is being a fan more important than anything else?

Using the word "fan" kind of turns a lot of people off. Everyone thinks that a fan is a "lower class" citizen—bullshit! A fan is someone who gives respect where respect is due, gives credit where credit is due and actually appreciates someone else's passion even if it's not their own. I'm a fan of anyone that has any type of passion, any type of fire within themselves because of a belief that they have. I might not believe in what they're doing, but if they're showing passion and they're on the money, they're going all the way with their shit, then I back that person even if I don't respect what they're going for. It's the crazy men, the not-normal citizens that will change the world and have changed the world throughout history—like Jesus, Ghandi, Moses, Martin Luther King Jr. and John Lennon. They're the people that came out, did things and said things knowing that they'd probably be murdered for what they did and said but they still did it and said it anyway. That just goes to show you. I'm not a firm believer in words written to me by other humans but I am a firm believer of life and individuality. Everyone has different thoughts and analogies for what I'm saying, yet it makes complete sense. They believed in what they did, and they did it. That's when you make an impact. Sometimes the impact is too powerful for the masses. There's a thought behind any expression, word or saying. It takes two seconds to realize if it's real or bullshit. Be yourself. Come up with your own way of doing the job you are destined to do. Sometimes the job you're destined to do isn't the one that you think you're destined to do. Doing what you think you're destined to do will take you to where you're destined to be. It is all a link. Just do it. Whatever you're doing in life, do it on your own road. Do not step on anyone else to get ahead. If you win and at the same time someone loses because you won, that makes you wicked. We have the capability of doing what we do, but it takes special people to be able to do it without affecting others. Don't skip over a chamber to get their first.

Matt Sorum
Drums
Velvet Revolver // Camp Freddy
Co-Founder – Sorum Noce
Previously: Guns N' Roses // The Cult

How has the music business changed since you started your career? What's your opinion on the changes?

The music, number one. The Internet, number two. The people that work at labels and in the business, number three. The fans have also changed. Radio's really changed. Touring has even changed. It's become a little bit of a monopoly. Companies like LiveNation and AEG own all of the venues and the radio stations so it's become a conglomerate. Everybody's in bed with each other, and it's incestual. I think traditionally music always has situations where it's become generic only because one person will have a hit with a certain genre of music, and then ten other bands would follow. Even during the time of Guns N' Roses, when that band hit, ten other bands came out wanting to look and sound like Guns N' Roses. After Nirvana hit, there was the grunge era. Even the disco era and heavy metal—when the hair bands hit, there were 20 hair bands. So now it's like pop music is the thing, but the problem with pop music is it's so generic that one band sounds like the other. You can't tell the difference. There are no real rock stars. The business has become a business where the people that run record companies know that bands are expendable. They can always go onto the next thing so they never get the chance to even develop a rock star. Nobody ever gets to show his face as rock star because the label's onto the next thing. They don't give a shit. They're the people in power, not the musicians. That's the sad state of affairs, man. It's just like the fucking world right now. The same shit's that going on in the world is the same shit that's going on in the music business.

What advice would you give to young aspiring industry-types? What qualities did you find comforting in writers, label people, publicists, etc?

Well, I have a publicist that I love, Mitch Schneider. He's a guy that's been around since David Bowie came into this. He's been doing this shit for a long time. He's old school. I believe what Mitch Schneider tells me. I don't believe a lot of other people. I have people that I surround myself with that I believe in. For a kid that's a musician, it's a scary idea and proposition to think about going to a record company—especially record companies who don't have much going on anymore. So if they're able to meet a guy like me who can give them advice, I'd say to them, "Look, be the best possible musician you can. Write the best songs you can. Be true to yourself. Don't buy into other people's fucking bullshit. Write the music that feels good to you, period. Move forward with it and try to change naturally and organically to suit yourself not other people." The kind of the people that shine through are artists like Prince and bands like Guns N' Roses, Nirvana, The Rolling Stones and Led Zeppelin. Why? Because they were original. Be original. The original guys that are great and talented will rise above everything. It's about the future. It's not about the fucking past. Listen to the past, but steer yourself towards the future. That's true for everyone in the music business.

What needs to happen for the industry to progress?

Somebody needs to come and shake fuckin' shit up and say, "You know what? Fuck this! We're not going to fucking buy into iTunes or any of this fucking conglomerate bullshit." Even though iTunes is the easiest way to get music, it's almost called the business because now look at those guys over at Apple. They're like, "You have to come to iTunes to get music." Bullshit! You could go to MattSorum.tv right now and download my shit or listen to it. So I think the way of the world is creative people like musicians need to say, "Look, we don't need any of you!" Musicians have to stand up for themselves. The problem with musicians is that they've always had a creative brain, and they've never had a business mind. That's the problem with artists. Artists get fucked because one side of their brains work, and one side doesn't. Generally, the creative side works, and the business side doesn't. So these people come in and they keep a lot of artists doped up, drugged up or alcohol-ed up, take advantage of them, discard them and move onto the next thing. It's the way of the world.

Is being a fan and having that passion more important than anything else?

I think passion is the number one goal in life, in general. If you're passionate about something, go for it—if you believe in yourself. Even when people try to tell you that you're not good enough or this, that or the other thing, believe in yourself and have the passion. It's always going to be hard knocks. Anything in life is. You have to respect yourself and know. Maybe you aren't the best, but at least believe that you are until you become the best. It's like my clothing line Sorum Noce. I don't know what the fuck I'm doing half the time [Laughs], but I believe in it, I have a passion for it and I love it. I have to see it through to fruition, if that takes me five years or ten. It could be ten years before I crack it with the clothing line but it's the same exact idea as being a musician. We're making a comeback. I'm talking to Velvet Revolver right now about how we're going to find another singer. Do I still want to do this? Am I passionate about it? Yes. That's passion and conviction. Hey man, I'm not going to lose. I'm not a loser. I'm going to win. Look, when I was a young musician and I went and saw Kiss for my first concert in 1975, I looked up onstage and I believed at that moment that I could be a rock star as good as those guys were. In my opinion, I was a really good drummer, but I was a fan of the music. At the same time, I thought to myself, "If those guys could do it, I could do it." It's just like a kid that looks up to Slash or any guitar hero. He sits in his room until he plays good enough. He says, "Fuck man, that guy's my icon and my idol, I aspire to be as good as he is." When you get to a point where maybe you are, it's time to step forward and go, "Look, I'm good enough to do this." It starts from being a fan though. Camp Freddy is the same idea. I'm a total fan of all those people

that we invite to play onstage with us. The fact that I've been onstage with Steven Tyler, Ozzy Osbourne, Billy Idol, Lemmy from Motorhead, The Sex Pistols and the list goes on and on. I was a fan of those bands. The fact that I'm standing next to them now is a dream come true, but that still resonates with me when I'm playing onstage with those guys. I'm like, "Wow, that's Jimmy Page and Robert Plant talking to me" or "Oh my God, I'm playing with Steven Tyler!"
At the same time I'm actually a peer with them now, I'm still a fan.

Wayne Static
Vocals & Guitar
Static-X

How has the music business changed since you started your career? What's your opinion on the changes?

The music business has completely changed since my first CD came out in 1999. At that time the internet and mp3 players were not much of a threat to CD sales. The internet was not even considered a promotional tool for the record companies then. Now it's the main focus for marketing, and in my opinion CD sales are no longer the measure of a band's success. Now days I would say a band is successful if they can support themselves touring. The CD has become less of a profitable product and more of a marketing tool to promote the live show, which is an experience that cannot be downloaded. I could write an entire book on how the industry has changed in nine years! MTV even played music videos back then! What a concept!

What advice would you give to young aspiring industry-types? What qualities did you find comforting in writers, label people, publicists, etc?

My advice to young aspiring industry types is to get into it for fun only, and don't expect to make any money at it. The industry is so unpredictable now. Very few people actually make a living in the music industry. And try to treat everyone you meet with respect, those people will remember how cool you are when the going gets tough and you need some help.

Where do you see the music industry going?

The trend I am seeing in the music industry is too many bands and less CD sales. It's so easy to promote your band on the internet, but then it's equally easy for everyone to steal your music. And with today's technology one kid can buy the CD and then all his friends can just burn a copy instead of buying it. I also predict a trend of the industry reverting back to the 1950's, when bands released singles instead of albums. Many people just buy the one song they like from iTunes instead of the entire record. This situation will lead to fewer mega-huge bands like Metallica and tons of underground bands. Whether this is good or bad depends on your perspective.

Is being a fan more important than anything else?

Being a music fan is absolutely the most important quality to possess if you want to make a name for yourself in the music industry. It takes years of hard work while making no money before anyone sees success. As long as you have a good time along the way then it's all worth it.

Troy Sanders
Vocals & Bass
Mastodon

What advice would you give to young aspiring industry-types? What qualities did you find comforting in writers, label people, publicists, etc?

Embody honesty 100%—pure and blatant honesty. Anything else is see-through, transparent bullshit that won't amount to a damn thing. If you're truly sincere about your art and how it's translated to the world, our music lives forever. No one wants this to be misinterpreted by any means! This is our band's state-ment—our life, our sacrifice and our ultimate mission. Any misconstrued information would be unaccept-able.

Where do you see the music industry going?
Thank Buddha, we tour our asses off, as that is the only means of loot and beans we will ever see!

Is being a fan more important than anything else?
To me, yes, being a fan is more important than all. I entered this choice as a fanatic lover of rock. Today, I remain maniacal toward my musical idols and heroes. Still being offered tours with our band's true musical deities—Black Sabbath, Slayer, Metallica, Tool and Iron Maiden—damnit, pinch me, I'm dreaming!

Jason Miller
Vocals & Guitar
Godhead

How has the music business changed since you started your career? What's your opinion on the changes?
It's changed quite a bit since I've been around, going from almost all physical to now a more and more digital world. A lot of hiccups in the industry have happened because of this, but I think that ultimately it will adapt and the best stuff will rise to the top. I know a lot of people are bitter about how the changes have affected them, but I try to keep a positive attitude about it. Even if the BUSINESS of music is in some turmoil, the act of MAKING music is alive and well, and thanks to technology, more accessible than ever.

What advice would you give to young aspiring industry-types? What qualities did you find comforting in writers, label people, publicists, etc?
Honesty. I love it when people are straight with me and don't try to promise me a million things or string me along. That pretty much goes across the board

Where do you see the music industry going?
I'm not sure. I've heard that large corporations will start sponsoring artists and record labels will disap-pear altogether. We're seeing some of that already but I also see that the independent artist can thrive even without a record label at all.

My thought is, if you put enough hard work into something and it's good, people will hear it.

Is being a fan more important than anything else?
REMEMBERING why you became a fan in the first place is more important than anything else.

Joby Ford
Guitar
The Bronx

How has the music business changed since you started your career? What's your opinion on the changes?
It has completely changed. It has become much smaller. The majority of people I knew that worked in music do not anymore. I would cite technology as the main factor. One person or a group can basically do the majority of what a record label can do right from their home computer these days.

What advice would you give to young aspiring industry-types? What qualities did you find comforting in writers, label people, publicists, etc?
I think people should always do what they want to do. If you want to write, write. Start a blog or a web site. Don't wait around for someone to offer you a job. Those are the kind of people that seem to still exist in today's musical climate—the ones that really love it and just do what they want to do, regardless of the paycheck. The other piece of advice is to embrace technology. It's not going to go away. If you can't beat them, join them.

Where do you see the music industry going?
Same place it always has been going—rich, old people hiring kids that love music to make them money. They hire kids that "have their finger on the pulse" because old dinosaurs have no taste—(see every major label closing down).

Is being a fan more important than anything else?
It depends on what you want. I imagine at some point every single person that works in this business is, was a fan. That's probably why they got into it. I think the most important thing is the actual music. I think it's a testament to how powerful music is— because every single thing about the music business blows: big ego label reps, journalists that feel that they can comment on someone's creativity even though they can't play a note of music (reminds me of a sports commentator), the people on the business side of things that have made stealing from your band par for the course and record producers who won't allow you to make the music you want to make because they have a reputation to uphold. The list goes on and on. So yes—the power of music is unstoppable and being a fan of that, even for a second, is the most important thing.

Paul Edge
DJ

How has the music business changed since you started your career? What's your opinion on the changes?

The biggest change has been the move from traditional mediums such as CDs and vinyl to digital downloads. Another major change is obviously the internet and its ability, when used properly, to promote new artists. Being a member of the "online generation," obviously I have welcomed these changes. The internet has leveled the playing field somewhat, allowing music to grow organically instead of as a result of massive hype. Added to this is the development of digital recording, that has resulted in a generation of musicians experimenting. Over the next 10 years I expect that the industry will start to not only appreciate the positive effect of the digital medium, but I also believe that music will evolve to previously unforeseen heights as the artistic limits of traditional instruments get replaced.

What advice would you give to young aspiring industry-types? What qualities did you find comforting in writers, label people, publicists, etc?

Don't let anyone tell you what to do, how to play, what to play and what to create. Never sell your soul for money, it reflects in your music. Innovate don't replicate. Be honest, have principles, keep your word and remember, if you are playing to a crowd of 1 or a crowd of 1000, you need to retain the same level of commitment, professionalism and artistic excellence for both.

I only ask for the following, that people I work with work as hard as I do, believe in the music I create, are genuinely honest and have integrity.

Where do you see the music industry going?

At this point I feel we will be seeing the emergence of a new breed of labels that understand the internet and can respond to the marketplace in a way that the monolithic majors cannot. I would like to think that the majors will eventually adapt as well. What we are witnessing at the moment is a tired and out-of-date paint-by-numbers template for bands, and the public are responding accordingly. Music should evolve, it is generational. Sociological things that affected my parents, also affected the musicians of their time, this was reflected in the music they made. In 2008, we are still seeing the basic band set up that was developed in the 1950s and the music, by definition, has not evolved with the times. I can write a song with 16 digitalized analog instruments and I have to play each instrument, write the chord sequences, etc. I then have to be the drummer and so on. However, because I am not writing music in the traditional way, I am deemed less talented than a guy who can only play the guitar. People's understanding of the complexities of writing music digitally need to change, people's expectations of what a "live show" is need to change, and in time they will. At that point the music industry will truly embrace the digital medium and the sky is the limit.

Is being a fan more important than anything else?

No.

Dani Filth
Singer
Cradle of Filth

How has the music business changed since you started your career? What's your opinion on the changes?

Our first album came out 15 years ago and that makes me want to rush out for wrinkle cream. In the 70s, you could get away with a 26 minute album. Nowadays, we have to pile it on. You need to think about when you go into the studio, don't overexert but write a few more songs that are probably necessary. Think about the long term, as well. Write 15 good songs instead of 10 good songs. Make sure demos are good. Kids like extra content, anyway, that you can include. Nowadays, the editions require so much more than they did before. There was money for bands back then before the variations like MVI, ringtones, downloads. There were 1,000 bands then. There are 100,000 now. It's swamped.

What advice would you give to young aspiring industry-types? What qualities did you find comforting in writers, label people, publicists, etc?

The business is cut throat, but I like more than anything, is when someone comes up to me out of the blue. When people chat your ear off, it can be fake. But when you have someone knowing what they are doing and not sucking up like a bloodthirsty vampire, do the research, be friendly. Be cordial. Those are the people that matter in the music business. It's a shark pool, isn't it? Get ahead, be a nice person. If you don't like the music, do the research and know their name and name check the songs.

Where do you see the music industry going?

There is over saturation so as a tip, you have to think of everything. Stand out in the crowd. So many bands rob someone else's sound but that doesn't work anymore. Spend all my money making a video for a good song, it's the way you will get noticed.
It's not gimmicky.

Is being a fan more important than anything else?

It's not the most important thing but is important to be a fan/ What's the point of being in the music business? If you work at Roadrunner, one would expect that you like some of the Roadrunner music. It's like being in a band. If you are not totally into what you are doing, just give up. It'd be pointless otherwise. The best window cleaners, I suspect, are those who like cleaning windows.

Dez Fafara
Vocalist
DevilDriver

How has the music business changed since you started your career? What's your opinion on the changes?

Downloading came along and now the business of music has felt the blow .

Record deals have dropped, record companies are doing what's called 360 deals which means they want 30% of your merch, publishing, and door take at your live shows in order for them to keep their big houses and fat salaries. Stay away from these deals!

This just starves out the humble musicians who no longer can tour and make money so they tour for nothing in support of a record that's making the company money not the musician. There are a flood of bands, more than ever fighting for the same place in music. Our economy going down has effected the marketplace with devastating consequences, both on those who would buy a record from an artist or pay 20 bucks for a ticket. How it has effected me? For anyone doing anything in art that's not mainstream,

especially music such as blues, jazz, punk or metal, downloading came in and now is threatening to put these categories of music in jeopardy since these artists survive on the fringe away from the "popular" stuff anyways. Hang in; it's gonna get rough!

What advice would you give to young aspiring industry-types? What qualities did you find comforting in writers, label people, publicists, etc?

For anyone entering into this works of art meets commerce, think art first.

Surround yourself with a good business manager, attorney, booking agent, management. All else will fall into place. Label people are the people within the company that work your record . Be professional around them.

Where do you see the music industry going?

One word: Digital

Is being a fan more important than anything else?

You must love what you do in this life. Life is too short to not follow your dreams and run against the wind . You must be a "fan" of the career choice you make or unhappiness will come haunting with quickness!

Herman Li
Guitarist
DragonForce

How has the music business changed since you started your career? What's your opinion on the changes?

The older and newer people need to adapt to what's going on right now. Everything is changing, it's a lot faster than it used to be, with the Internet is working and the industry is driven by the technology more than ever before. Somehow it's hard to predict what will happen but everything needs to be looked at again. It's so fast and music business people have to keep their eyes open.

What advice would you give to young aspiring industry-types? What qualities did you find comforting in writers, label people, publicists, etc?

The computer will rule the world for the next 100 years. And you are at a disadvantage if you don't have one. You will be way behind. Songwriting, record label, you have to relate to it. You can't expect things to happen for you.

Where do you see the music industry going?

I see the strong surviving and those who don't care won't and they will spend all their money instead of learning for themselves, which they should. No one can really tell where it will end up. Information just moves too fast with technology anymore.

Is being a fan more important than anything else?

Being a fan is most important, yes. It's one thing.

Paul Gargano
Writer
Manager

How has the music business changed since you started your career? What's your opinion on the changes?

The most obvious changes in the music industry over the past two decades have been the consolidation of major labels and the emergence of the Internet as a marketing tool. On the positive side, it has become much easier for young bands to expose their music to more widespread audiences. A negative is the absolute over-saturation of the industry. With the emergence of other entertainment mediums, and more competition for money and attention, the results are a much smaller piece of the pie for artists and bands. The end result? It's easier and more economical than it's ever been to make music and get music to the people. That said, and taking into account the ever-rising costs of gas, it's harder than it's ever been to sustain that music on the road. The music industry is at a crossroads.

What advice would you give to young aspiring industry-types? What qualities did you find comforting in writers, label people, publicists, etc?

The biggest piece of advice I would offer is simply to step back and realize the magnitude and scope of what you're hoping to achieve in the music industry, and why you hope to achieve it. There are more bands out there than there are people working for them, which means, mathematically, it's easier to make it in a band than it is to make it in the business side of the music industry. Know what you're getting into. Much like America, the landscape is lopsided—the top 10% make all the money, while the remaining 90%, for the most part, work longer hours than they'd like to, and make less money than they'd make for comparable work in other fields. If it isn't a labor of love, it becomes a labor of fruitless frustration, so make sure the love is there. Since working in the music industry means that most of your friends come from the music industry, I look for the same qualities in both: Warmth, charm, happiness and honesty.

A little humility also goes a long way. And please be able to talk about something other than music every once in a while. Imagine working at McDonalds and people only wanting to talk about French fries and Happy Meals all day…

Where do you see the music industry going?

If I knew the answer to that, I'd have started MySpace! The music industry being a microcosm of the world we leave in, things need to bottom out before they get better. I'd like to think that things can't get much worse, but there's always someone out there all too willing to prove me wrong. People say fresh blood is the answer, but I think it's a combination of fresh blood with old blood, so a new outlook can be embraced by the existing foundation. I think bands are going to be forced to become more and more reliant on themselves to create a core, because there just isn't enough money to go around when it comes to hangers on and flashy habits. From there, the right partnerships will promote healthy growth and prosperity. But only once the foundation is established.

Is being a fan more important than anything else?

No. While being a fan of music is extremely important and remembering why you became a fan is just as important, it's equally important to remember that the minute you start working from inside the machine, you become a cog in the wheel that makes the industry go round. At that point, you're part of the business of music and you can't let being a fan cloud those mechanics. That's one of the reasons why the industry isn't for everybody: While it's critical to be a fan, it's just as crucial to be objective. As in life, balance is key.

Mike Gitter
A&R
RoadrunnerRecords

How has the music business changed since you started your career? What's your opinion on the changes?

It's shrunk. It's had to become more self-aware of it's own economics. It's no longer top-heavy -- record deals are no longer as over-the-top and enormous as they once were. They're no longer predicated on the expectation of hundreds of thousands of sales. Artists are rarely in a position to demand the sun, the moon and the stars -- unless of course, they're already established. It makes sense that the cultural and business excesses of the late eighties and early nineties have become streamlined. They've had to be.

Bluntly, we're selling fewer records. Way less records. Why? Sure, downloading. We live in the age of transparency and for the average Joe, why not get something for nothing? But beyond that, there's a lot of shitty records out there. Why take a $15 shot on something you're not sure of? Remember, in one's hierarchy of needs, buying a record comes somewhat after food, shelter and clothing. Also, music is in competition with other media. Video games, DVD's—even home computers. Go into a Best Buy and you'll see the music section shrinking while these other categories are growing like crazy.

The media outlets are extremely different now. MTV is less of a force than it's ever been. In the early 90's, a "Buzz Clip" was a quick conduit to an easy 100K sold. Now, that programming has been replaced by *The Hills* and stuff that has very little to do with music! Enter You Tube or MySpace. Are these as effective tools? Do they reach the casual fan? Probably not. You already have to be a fan to checking the stuff out. Also, let's not make light of the fact that the economy is tightening like a noose. The average Schmoe ain't got the Kizash.

So let's assess these changes and how we move into the future. I have a very strong belief that the record business is in trouble but the music business is actually OK. People still go see live music. People still buy merchandise. So, for better or worse, this has forced the record companies to forge "partnerships" with their artists commonly referred to as "360 Deals" where they participate and in theory help foster the artist's business. It's a good model if acted upon equally by both parties. Does this mean the nature of our careers in music can potentially change? Absolutely. The key to survival is adaptation, mutation and evolution. OK, so call me a mutant!

What advice would you give to young aspiring industry-types? What qualities did you find comforting in writers, label people, publicists, etc?

As trite as it sounds - be real. Have fun. Don't become jaded or cynical about something as fun as working with music. And most importantly, always value your position as a person lucky enough to work with something you're passionate about: music. Great music and great people in music always come from the streets. Like I've said before -- it isn't a job; it's a lifestyle and that passion should extend into your professional life.

Now, all that said, take that enthusiasm and push yourself to be a passionate "pro." There's nothing better than someone who is all about the rock who also gets the business side of the music business—who can somehow reconcile being a fan and being a professional. The best way you can help the music and the artists that you are so into and so enthusiastic about is by pushing yourself to understand the age old push and pull between art and commerce.

Now, for all you writer types, and I'm sure most of you saw the movie *Almost Famous*. There's that great bit at the beginning with Phillip Seymour Hoffman as Lester Bangs telling the kid to not buy into or necessarily trust the music machine and the slick sales tactics that go along with it. Let's face it: it is advertising. One of the biggest reasons I got out of "rock journalism" was that I felt that it wasn't really journalism per-se but a very subtle kind of ass-kissing and servitude where mediocrity is hailed and backs are slapped. And for many journalists and magazines, it's about access and ego-stroking. Remember that as you go down that road. Like ol' Lester said: "These people are not your friends."

Where do you see the music industry going?

Well, the music business is perfectly fine. People still come out to see bands play and buy merchandise. It's the record business that's having problems. There's still gold in them thar hills, Jethro. But it really comes down to how you mine it. The way I see it, record companies aren't necessarily record companies. They're lifestyle companies, branding companies and the bigger over-companies like Warner or Sony are even bigger lifestyle companies, the total picture of which is made up by an aggregation of these smaller labels. OK, so you've heard about the 360 deal, the theoretical partnership between artist and label where both parties share in all aspects of a band's career and income streams -- records, publishing, merchandise and live business. If this is in fact a true partnership, it is a really good situation where the artist can grow its business and the label participates in the benefits of their investment and hard work. This can also involve such things as fan clubs or something very significant on the publishing side: extensive and aggressive foreign collection. OK, so where is it all going? I'm not about to sound the death knell anytime soon. It's really down to recognizing that there is still money and great music to be made. If we're smart about it, we'll still have jobs and continue to do something we truly love.

Is being a fan more important than anything else?

At the end of the day, if you aren't a fan, then what's the point? This is just as much a lifestyle as it is a business. Sure, there are plenty of widget-producing drones involved in the music biz–exactly like any other business—but what's the point? Those are the people you see come and go. The great legends of the music business started out as fans. Jimmy Iovine starting off in a mailroom. Hell, the biggest example being Ahmet Erteghun, the founder of Atlantic Records, the guy who found and signed a little band called Led Zeppelin and discovered most of what modern rock, jazz and blues is founded upon. He did start Atlantic with his brother out if his passion for jazz. And of course, the great independent labels of our day: Epitaph, Sub-Pop, Touch & Go, Metal Blade were all started by people who were in love with music and selflessly wanted to embrace and promote it. And, of course, most of them initially lost a lot of money but didn't really care. Then again, how much money have we all invested in records, concert tickets, t-shirts over the years? The mind boggles! How can you not be a fan and get into music as a career? If it wasn't for being mesmerized by those first few Aerosmith and Zeppelin records which eventually led to Devo and Black Flag, I doubt I'd be doing this. I've always figured that if you didn't embrace sports it was rock n roll. For me, those records and the rush of seeing bands live in my teenage years definitely made you feel like you belonged somewhere. Way too many decades later, the sense of cultural belonging still carries on. Shit, how can you hang with someone who doesn't own *Houses of the Holy* or *I Against I*? Impossible! Yes, I sound like John Cusack in *High Fidelity*—a movie so fucking close to reality it hurts. So just to go back to that thought about journalism...

It's like the kid in *Almost Famous* is warned about by none other than Lester Bangs and ultimately finds to be true....THE PEOPLE ARE NOT YOUR FRIENDS...rock journalism has so been beaten broken and compromised, it might as well be a freelance means of writing press releases. The minute "honesty" comes into the equation, the minute you have to tell it like it is–a piece of crap record is, well, a piece of steaming monkey poop, you're persona non-grata. The rock press at this point—and there are notable and thankful exceptions—if glorified advertising. The minute an artist of record company's bubble is popped, forget about the notion of "access." They're going to find going to find someone more sycophantic and toss you to the side of the road like a used Durex condom. Or what's worse is the notion of ferreting out the heretical from the beginning. I can think of one case where a formerly underground band would not allow a couple journalists who long knew and supported them to write about their supposed jump to "major" territory. The rationale? It might run counter to a new image or sound they were trying to dupe new fans into believing came out of the ether. Ah, how you can be the powerful and the pariah in the same day! But then again, I've been on both sides of the desk. As a label, you desperately want to protect months of hard work, creativity and ego. You can almost understand those hip-hop style beatdowns at the offices of *Vibe*. And you thought writing about your favorite bands was going to be fun? Sorry kiddies, it's a dangerous, ugly business.

Bob McLynn
Manager
Bassist

How has the music business changed since you started your career? What's your opinion on the changes?

People don't buy records anymore. That's a big change! It sucks, but people will still need new music and we'll find new ways to make a living with it. In management we work with touring, merch, etc. We don't rely only on album sales so as long as we work with bands that can tour we will be fine.

What advice would you give to young aspiring industry-types? What qualities did you find comforting in writers, label people, publicists, etc?

Get out and do something. Go on tour or book shows in your local area. Immerse yourself in the music scene, make friends, and find a way you can work with local artists. That's how you learn, not in school.

Where do you see the music industry going?

Artists that can tour will survive. the ones that rely on a big song here and there will go by the wayside. In a perfect world, you have touring artists that have big hits. There aren't going to be big upfront deals anymore. Go out and prove it and make money when you do.

Is being a fan more important than anything else?

Yes, you need to love what you do or you wont be any good at it

Monte Conner
A&R
Roadrunner Records

How has the music business changed since you started your career? What's your opinion on the changes?

It's scary since I've been doing this a long time so my whole perception of the music business is based on the past, with physical units. It is changing over to digital. Kids aren't interested in physical product any longer. I know music as physical stores, going to Tower Records and hanging out and browsing and meeting other people doing the same thing because they are into music. That is what I love and why I got into the music business. A guy like me is going to be negative and think it's for the worst because what I love is changing and my world is changing. I am not the right guy to ask. If you talk to someone who is 18 or just started, he would be able to go on the Internet and have all these unsigned bands at his fingertips. He will say its better than ever, there are more files going around. That's my experience, as a consumer. I am a consumer still. I don't feel it is as good. I don't like the fact that you can't go into a record store and there is zero mystique to a band. When I was 14 in 1977, I got into Aerosmith because I heard "Walk This Way" on the radio. There was no way to hear Aerosmith. You couldn't see a video on MTV. You couldn't go buy a DVD or a VHS and watch them. You couldn't go online and research them. If you were creative, you could email them these days. The only way to find out about them was to hope *Circus* or *Hit*

Parader did a story on them! Or if they came to town. And even then, tickets were hard to come by, you are 14, parents won't take you, you miss out on tickets. There was a mystique and you craved information and every piece you got was amazing. I never saw Aerosmith in the flesh and when I saw them was a TV special, California Jam 2. We gathered in front of the TV and watched 10 bands and we were all bug-eyed watching these bands since there was no video on You Tube. It was done in a heartbeat and gone forever. It was such a mystique that made music so special. That is gone. It is so easy and rampant nowadays. It doesn't mean as much. There is no quality control. Before, you save your allowance and spend five dollars on an Aerosmith album. Now you can go online and steal 100 albums or get files sent by your friends. The whole thing has gone to shit for me. I can see why young kids and a new generation love the way it is. To them, they get more music and its free.

What advice would you give to young aspiring industry-types? What qualities did you find comforting in writers, label people, publicists, etc?

I would say if you are going to work in music business is to be a music freak. People who work here work long hours. To me, it helps if you are a freak for music. Sometimes we don't realize that. Sometimes dealing with my boss, the guy you don't want to piss off but at the heart of it, I see him read a Clash article, one of his favorite bands and he gets all giddy. We are all the same. He is doing this because he was like me in college. We become adults and don't realize and forget that they were teenagers who loved music, too. That is the number one quality. IF you want to work with it 24/7, then you have to. Advice I have is to be truthful and tell it like it is. Don't have an ego, despite your success. Be yourself and treat people as fellow human beings with respect and you will be successful. Even if you get to a "level," don't be an asshole.

Where do you see the music industry going?

There will always be a music business of some sort. It may shrink massively to a smaller business. There will be an infrastructure as long as there is money to be made. There will always be bands making music and kids wanting the music these bands make. It can continue as a business but the current business model, with labels selling physical units for profit, that model is broken and there is yet to be a new model that has emerged. The digital sales are up, but they are not nearly enough to make up for what is being lost. It keeps falling and digital is not picking up the slack. It's less than half of what's been lost. I don't know the new business model but I am sure we will see it. It is a difficult period right now. Labels will go under and there will be less job opportunities.

Is being a fan more important than anything else?

I do. That is a primary reason to work in this business but what people do not realize, especially in A&R, you have to continue to delicately walk a fine line between art and commerce. There are tons of bands I love. One of my favorite bands is Fu Manchu. I love that band. I have had opportunities to sign them over the years, but I cannot do it just because I am a fan. As great as love Fu Manchu is, I have to look at the business reality and the style of music they play is not a mass appeal style that sells a lot of records. It's really niche and it's hard to make money, so I have had to resist the urge to sign one of my favorite bands. You have to think of the business side of things and when I was starting, I didn't know that. I was young, dumb and full of cum. I did not have the experience to understand what my market was. I wanted to sign whatever I liked. I had to gain experience and it's not all about what I like. That's part of it and in a perfect world, you should be able to sign stuff you like but I have passed on signing things I liked because it wasn't a good business move. And I have signed things I didn't 100 percent love, but it was a good business move.

I would never sign something I hated. I may have lowered my standards a bit. The bottom line is you have to have some passion.

Mitch Schneider
President
MSO (Mitch Schneider Organization)

How has the music business changed since you started your career? What's your opinion on the changes?

I think the biggest change has to be the Internet and how we do business. While of course you still talk to people, but the majority of your work these days is reaching out to the media—me being a publicist—through the Internet. My advice to young people would be, you'd better at least minor in English because if you can't compose an email or appear grammatically proficient, you'll be mocked—maybe not openly mocked. However, on all these big group emails, where people hit "Reply to all," you should know the difference between the words "affect" and "effect." You should know the difference between the possessive "its" or when you're saying, "it is," which is "it's." I say all these kinds of things, and you get to see who's educated and who isn't. So the Internet is a big thing right there. In terms of how we can reach out to the media, I can now include mp3s in our pitches, links to bands' MySpace pages so a journalist who may not have the time to rip open the package that we just sent them might be able to just click on a link and hear something, and he or she might go, "This band sounds cool, maybe I should really open that CD." I think that's where it's amazing. Those kinds of changes are really positive for the business because our job as publicists is to get people interested in something. In the old days, we'd send out packages, and I'd put foil packages in there. It used to work. People would say, "Mitch, we found your advance CD right away because you sent it in a foil envelope." It's about doing things like that because as a publicist what you really want to do is stop the traffic. You want to get people's attention because that's what we do for a living. With the Internet now, journalists are receiving hundreds of emails, but hopefully you can compose a good email, you know how to be smart and you know how to pitch really fast. When I do my voice pitches—we used to leave pitches as voicemail before email—I used to have a really great 20-second description of a band's music or the angle of why I was calling because people would just hit "delete" otherwise. It's the same thing with an email. If your email is too long, the journalist will just hit "delete." I really try to be sensitive to those aspects. For me, that's a big change in the music industry. Fortunately, live music is more pervasive than ever. If you were to open up an issue of *La Weekly* or a weekly in any city in America, there are probably more pages advertising music gigs than there were five years ago. I attribute that to the fact that there used to be more singles heard on the radio and there were more videos played on MTV. With reality T.V. having upstaged music videos on a lot of channels, bands have to get their music out to people and one of the ways to do that is to play live. There are bands that come through any city in America, at least in Los Angeles, five times on one album. They'll start out on a small gig, moving up to the larger venue, then sometimes bands will end at a smaller venue. Let's say you have a name-platinum band. They're going to do the pre-release gig at the Avalon or the Wiltern. Then comes the Staples Center gig. Maybe that band comes back, and they're on a festival. Then they come back when the album's winding down, and it's like a goodbye and they go back to a smaller venue. It's like, "See you next time!" I think it's different. Musicians have to stay on the road longer than they ever planned on. In the old days, people would be purchasing your music more. Now people are getting it for free online. Before, your video would be on MTV. You'd be on the radio, and you'd see the difference. Now, you've got to stay on the road if you want to get people into your music. You want to sell t-shirts and merch because you're not making that money in CDs anymore. The more you gig, the more people will come to your shows and buy your t-shirts. I think musicians have it rougher than they ever have. That's my little take on the music business.

When I was growing up, people would say, "Mitch, did you ever see that band?" Well, "No, they only came through my city twice on an album cycle." If you had plans, that date might not have matched up with your schedule. Now, these bands come through and you can see them. Maybe they're on the *Warped Tour* or *Coachella*. As a fan, you have more access to living, breathing music than ever before in history.

The press matters more than it ever has as well. In the '80s and maybe the '90s as well to a certain degree, I think a lot of artists got used to their videos being played on video channels. They got used to their music being heard on the radio. Now, the press matters more than it ever has. You may have to open up a magazine whether its *Spin*, *Blender*, *RollingStone* or *Alternative Press* not to mention various Internet outlets that will give you information, and you will rely on what's buzzing. You'll need to check out *Spin.com*'s "Hot Band of the Day." It's different, and I think the press does matter more than ever.

What advice would you give to young aspiring industry-types? What qualities did you find comforting in writers, label people, publicists, etc?

I think that you have to live and breathe music if you're planning on getting into the music industry. You have to be really open to different genres of music. It's just not enough saying you just like hard rock or whatever. You have to be pretty fluent saying something like, "I like indie rock, and that also encompasses noise rock." If you like metal, then you should know about hardcore and post-hardcore. You should know a little bit about electronic music as well. Knowing this is really key. I think people should be subscribing to magazines. Yes, everything's online, but there's nothing like sitting down with a copy of *RollingStone* or another magazine and really getting a feeling for it. That's really important. That's what I like to see from people who come in here—somebody who can say, "I dig Yeasayer, Crystal Method and As I Lay Dying." That's what it takes. You have to be really well-rounded. You can't say you just like classic rock and a couple new bands. You've got to know all of it. If you take a journalist out to lunch, you're not going to only pitch your bands. That writer might say, "I've been listening to the new Raphael Saddiq album." It's like, "Yeah, you should know about that." Neo-soul, or whatever you want to call it. You have to be able to converse otherwise you're seen as just stumping for your own band. That's not attractive. I think journalists want to see publicists who are passionate, smart and knowledgeable. That's important.

When people ask me what I do for a living, I say, "Well, I'm a publicist, but I can tell you what I do. I put vibe into a bottle and I spray the universe with it." That's how I look at what I do. I get to be a DJ to a certain degree. How do I turn people onto this so they come to the gig, spin the CD and write about the band? Creative ideas for new bands and classic bands are crucial. In MSO's very long run with KoRn, we constantly came up with ideas that made them very appealing. On their last album *See You On the Other Side*, after the album came out, management was looking to come up with a campaign to give some heft to the fact that the band was going to be launching a major tour. So we sat around and brainstormed. We said, "Well, the album's called *See You On the Other Side*, maybe we can do a press conference announcing the tour at a cemetery?" It played off the title. So we did a grave side press conference, and that morphed into an evening party at the Mausoleum at the *Hollywood Forever* Cemetery. Axl Rose actually came to that party. That was his first sighting in five years, and when Axl Rose shows up at your party when he's been absent for so long, everybody in the press was just buzzing, "Oh the KoRn party, Axl Rose came." Aside from it being a great party for KoRn, we had that extra celebrity factor that gave the party more dimension and thus generated more column inches in the press and on web sites across the country.

KoRn still have great management with Jeff Kwatinez and Peter Katsis at The Firm. They really pushed us to keep delivering creative ideas even including their *Family Values* tour brand. *Family Values* did a ten-dollar ticket in 2006. So we came up with this crazy idea that Jonathan Davis was going to be in Chicago after a Cubs game, and we set up a mini *Warped Tour*-style stage and he met all the fans. Then we brought a big mechanical fan on stage. Jonathan Davis had 10,000 dollars in his hands and he just put it up against the fan. 10,000 dollars just blew out into the crowd. That was our way to drive this interest in the fact that there were $10 tickets. He had 10,000 dollars in $10 bills floating out into this sea of people. We got huge press on that as well. There was always something with KoRn that was fun and notable. The band has a great sense of humor in addition to their dark and unsettling music. There's that fun side to them, and I think MSO definitely helped play a part in putting that out there to the public and thus to their fans.

3. Where do you see the music industry going?

I think what we're seeing right now in America is the explosion of live music—not only in these multiple gigs I mentioned previous. You're also seeing something that I would call, "Festival Culture." I'm talking about everything from *Coachella* and *Bonnaroo* to *Voodoo Music Experience* and *Austin City Limits*. I think as the Internet galvanizes and people are stuck in that cyber community they want to go out more. Festivals have become a meeting ground for people. Fans also have a choice of 120 bands to see in one weekend. Not that they could see every one, but that choice is available. I think we're going to continue to see festival culture have a good run. Not only because of the diversity and people wanting to interact with each other as human beings, but it's also financially doable. You can buy a one-day ticket and experience ten hours of music. Festival culture's big, so I think we're going to see that. If I had that crystal ball, I'd be able to say, "Oh, there's going to be a new show called *American Idol* [Laughs." That's already here. I think more bands are going to come up with new ways to expose their music. We handle Smashing Pumpkins. They've left the major label system by their own design, and their new single is going to be available via *Guitar Hero*. They're the first band to release a new song exclusively through the game. I think you're going to see bands come up with more scenarios like that. You have a classic band like AC/DC putting their album out exclusively through Wal Mart because that's where they believe their people are, and they're getting incredible promotion through Wal Mart. We saw that worked for The Eagles. I think you're going to see bands come up with dynamic retail scenarios so they can actually sell their music because at this point, we're saying the closure of record stores continuing, and that's how the business is going to work. You're going to see more "events," like AC/DC and Wal Mart, Aerosmith with their own game and the Pumpkins on *Guitar Hero*. You're going to continually see these sorts of scenarios develop.

With so much music out there, the industry has to produce events to focus the public's attention. That's what's going to happen.

Is being a fan more important than anything else?

I don't know if I want to say it's more important than anything else because you could have someone whose a massive fan but he or she hasn't mastered certain techniques like English [Laughs]. You have to be able to compose great emails. You have to understand that an office begins at a certain time, and you have to show up on time. To get a job in the music business, all these things are important—being fluent with the English language, being hardworking and diligent coupled with the fact that you're a music connoisseur. That's what I think you need to be. People can see that you really mean it. I really look for that in the kinds of employees we have here. I want to make sure they're connoisseurs. I want MSO's client list to be just like somebody's iPod. There are some groovy PR agencies in New York that are like 95 percent alternative music, and that's all well and fine, but I think the really great thing about MSO is in one day we signed Dropkick Murphys and Dolly Parton. I said, "That's the kind of company that I'd want to work for because that's what it's all about." Be a music connoisseur be really discerning and be somebody whose really well-read. Buy books. There are so many artists who have written some really great books on the music business and their experiences. Read all that stuff. A great book a like to recommend is *So You Wanna Be a Rock and Roll Star* by Jacob Slichter. He used to be the drummer for Semisonic, and it's a really good look at the life of that band. It talks about how MCA had to pump a million dollars into that song "Closing Time" in order to make it a hit. It just goes into what that band had to do—moving from a band to a bus, and it's like the world through their eyes. I tell people at MSO you really need to read that book so when you're with a musician you understand the world through their eyes.

Good example: in the book, Jacob talks about how they're at the Conan show, and it's all new to them. When I read that, I thought it was interesting because I cover my bands all the time, but I just walk-in and figure in my head, "We've all done this before." No. This could be a band's first shot on *The Tonight Show*. So now I try to be a little more sensitive when I walk into a room and I say, "If you have a moment, let me just lay out the day for you and how it's going to work. By the way, *The Tonight Show* has an average of four million viewers per night. You guys are going to go in the last 15 minutes of the show. There's makeup. There's a commissary over there to get food." A road manager says a lot of this, but you can personalize it as a publicist, and say, "Other bands that have been on the show this week were Von Bondies and Beyonce." So the band feels like they're doing a great show and it's a big moment for them. I try to personalize it so the band can feel a part of it. For instance when you go on *The Tonight Show*, in the morning there's a sound check and at one o'clock they do an on-camera rehearsal. For a new band, it all goes really fast. So we tell our bands, "If you're going to do something at a taping do it at the on-camera rehearsal so the camera knows that you're going to jump off an amplifier." If you do that at a taping, but the director didn't know about it, he may not even get that shot. I try to tell this band, "This is what's going to happen." I'm such a fan of the music that I really care about it and I want to tell the bands this. That's how I work.

The press does make a difference. Because there's so much music right now, you need a filter to help you. It's not only like listening to something on the radio. What shows did the *LA Weekly* pick this week? *RollingStone* does a hot list, "songs that our editors are playing this week." You need somebody to condense it. 30,000 albums are released in a year, who could even deal with that? We look for these filters, so the press does matter.

Kristine Ashton-Magnuson
Senior Vice President
MSO (Mitch Schneider Organization) 1995-present
Levine/Schneider PR 1992-1995
(when MSO broke off from the company to focus on music publicity)

How has the music business changed since you started your career? What's your opinion on the changes?

When I first got into the music industry as an intern at Levine/Schneider PR in 1992, labels had a lot more money to spend on expensive parties, press dinners and other events. Things have definitely changed since then due to all of the budget cutbacks. In addition, in order for a band to sign to a label, having contacts in the industry was much more important than it is today. Indie labels, social networking sites like MySpace and grassroots tours like the Vans Warped Tour, Taste Of Chaos Tour, etc. have opened up new opportunities for bands to put out a record and tour. With these types of opportunities available to them, many bands are able to sustain themselves even without signing to a label. For example, a new band can create a huge following through MySpace. Kevin Lyman and the Vans Warped Tour have also broken many baby bands by giving them an opportunity to perform on the tour after displaying a strong work ethic, musical talent and progression in their development. The "lifestyle" aspect of the music industry definitely plays a stronger role than it has in the past as well. In the 90s (and of course prior to that time as well), radio and CD sales could make or break a band, while a band can now become successful through building their own fan base via touring, online marketing, press, etc.

Publicity has also changed in many ways. When I started in the business, there was no such thing as an online publication. Media outlets were much more limited and were comprised of print magazines, newspapers and fanzines, along with TV outlets. With the rise of the internet, online publications play a substantial role in many artists' press campaigns. There are also many more opportunities for bands to receive press coverage due to the increase in number of outlets. The value of publicity has increased, since radio and video opportunities for bands are more limited.

What advice would you give to young aspiring industry-types? What qualities did you find comforting in writers, label people, publicists, etc?

I'd definitely recommend doing at least one internship, if you're interested in the music business. This will give you a taste of the different aspects of the music industry and will also provide invaluable experience. Many companies will not hire someone who does not have some sort of experience in the industry and also look to their intern pool when hiring assistants. I personally started my career as an intern, was hired as receptionist and then worked my way up from assistant, to Tour Publicist and eventually Senior Vice President during my 16 years at MSO (which spun off from Levine/Schneider PR in 1995).

As far as qualities I admire in writers, label people and publicists, I enjoy working with people who are good communicators and like working as a team. When you're in the business of communication, it's important to respond to emails and phone calls in a timely manner, whether you're dealing with an important manager or a small online fanzine. I also respect those who are organized and dedicated to their work. As a music publicist, it's important to remember that the amount of effort you put into a project can contribute to that artist's success or failure.

Where do you see the music industry going?

It seems as if things are falling more and more into the hands of the artists to independently oversee and/or handle everything from publicity to distribution to marketing. The previous major label business model seems like it's being phased out and altered since bands are not able to sell as many CDs as they used to. While the major labels have had to adopt new strategies, big business is still a force in the music industry. Consolidation of ownership in other areas of the industry has limited artists' access to radio, video, and touring opportunities--so publicity, grassroots marketing, and finding alternate means of reaching an audience are increasingly important for emerging artists.

Digital music is become more and more prevalent and bands now make a bulk of their income from touring and merchandise, rather than CD sales. I think the shift will continue in the direction of digital music taking over and bands becoming even more independent and involved in guiding their own careers.

Is being a fan more important than anything else?

If you want to get into the music industry, I think it's very important that you're a music fan. While there are some high paying careers in this field, most everyone starts from the bottom (as an intern or assistant) and gradually works their way up. A career in the music industry generally involves a lot of hours (sometimes at a low wage), so you need to be passionate about your work in order to be successful. As a publicist, you may also encounter lots of rejection along the way--some journalists ultimately will not like the band you're pitching them and artists may not always like what the press write about them--so it's crucial that you maintain a positive attitude and focus on celebrating the successes of your efforts.

James Patrick
Manager
Fox Music

How has the music business changed since you started your career? What's your opinion on the changes?

From the film music perspective, not much has changed in terms of how we do things from a production standpoint. Other than music supervisors getting more clout because A&R is pretty much going the way of the Dodo bird. But one of the biggest changes we've seen is the steady decline in soundtrack sales. When I was a kid, buying soundtracks was the way to go, because spending 15 bucks on a CD with one or two good tracks wasn't exactly cheap. Now with the digital age upon us, people can either go to iTunes or steal songs off file sharing sites, practically making the traditional soundtrack obsolete. Needless to say, this is putting a lot of people out of work.

What advice would you give to young aspiring industry-types? What qualities did you find comforting in writers, label people, publicists, etc?

Be that person who thinks outside the box because that's what it's going to take in 2009. Know what you want. The sooner you know the direction you want to go, the better. Pay attention to new media and all it encompasses. The problem with the music biz is that people are still doing things the way they did them 10 years ago. You, the aspiring industry type... Think about how people will be doing things 10 years from now. That's what will make you a step ahead of the rest.

Where do you see the music industry going?

The Record industry is quickly dying. Artists have reached a point where they don't care if people steal their music online because they know they'll get it back in touring (i.e. Lars Ulrich's recent comments about the leak of the new Metallica album). But what that's doing is creating more losses in revenue for the labels, causing them to let more people go. The labels aren't going to suffer, that's what the minions are for. No, it's going to take some 19 year old kid in college who comes up with an idea that anyone over 30 couldn't even begin to imagine. That's what it's going to take. I predict a major label to crumble in the next 5 years and those tied to the business know exactly which label I'm referring to.

Is being a fan more important than anything else?

If we weren't fans then why are we dong what we do? For the money? There's no money in this biz unless you're above the line so it's all about being a fan and having a love and passion for Music. I was both a fan of film and music, What better then a career that involves both?

Ashley White
Director of Publicity
Atlantic Records

How has the music business changed since you started your career? What's your opinion on the changes?

The music business has changed tremendously since I started my career. Even small details in the day to day operations: I remember as an intern, eight years ago, the phone in the publicity department of a major label literally did not stop ringing. The day consisted of answering phones, and it was impossible to keep up with them. Yet email has now (thankfully) alleviated the incessant ringing. Of course, there are much larger changes. I've weathered several mergers and company consolidations. I've seen countless peers at all different types of music-related companies lose their jobs but then find their way, some staying in music, some deciding it's time to leave. I truly believe it's all just a series of growing pains. There will always be music fans, and, consequently, there will always be a music business to serve those fans. The disc may become an mp3 file, the magazine may become a blog, the concert may become a podcast, but there will always be someone listening, reading, and watching.

What advice would you give to young aspiring industry-types? What qualities did you find comforting in writers, label people, publicists, etc?

Never stop loving music and loving what you do. Be in this industry because you can't see yourself doing anything else. You will know very quickly if this is where you really want to be.

As far as qualities in other writers, label people, etc., I would say follow the Golden Rule. Everyone has bad days. Just treat people fairly, the way you'd want them to treat you. Inevitably, everything comes full circle in this business. The people you help today will be there for you tomorrow, when you're asking for their help.

Where do you see the music industry going?

I see there being more and more opportunities within the music industry for all types of artists. The Internet has obviously made music more readily available, and it has also given music fans thousands of new ways to discover new music. No longer do you have to wait at the bookstore or record store for the latest issue of your favorite music magazine, or only listen to the one rock radio station in your town to hear anything new. Fans can read about and hear music everywhere online, and discover artists much more easily than ever before. This has, in a sense, created less massive superstars, as there are fewer huge mainstream outlets. But the smaller, more niche outlets have built a generation of artists for every fan. No matter how specific your taste in music is, there is something out there for you. And, unlike 10 years ago, you can very easily find and purchase it.

Is being a fan more important than anything else?
Yes. Everyone in the music industry will at some point work on a project that isn't their favorite. But having a passion for music will drive you every day, in projects you love and projects you might not. Seeing people be passionate about your artists and knowing firsthand the connection that they feel as fans always brings you back to why you do what you do everyday.

Benjie Gold
Right Lane Ends Management

How has the music business changed since you started your career? What's your opinion on the changes?
The music business is completely different than it was just 10 years ago. It used to be a business about selling LPs. Cassettes, CDs, etc. Artist development was essential to help build a band. It would sometimes take 4 or 5 albums for a band to have success. The music business used to actually care about the music. Now it is turning into style over substance, and mediocrity is accepted. The music business has shifted. The days of selling CDs are gone, but touring, merchandising, licensing are still ways that bands are making money. Licensing used to be something that artists frowned up because it potentially could show you as a "sell out," now artists are whoring themselves out for survival.

What advice would you give to young aspiring industry-types? What qualities did you find comforting in writers, label people, publicists, etc.?
Go to college and find something else to do.

Where do you see the music industry going?
I said this in the answer to question one.

Is being a fan more important than anything else?
I think so, but unfortunately as with any other job or career, if it feels like work, it is not exciting. Passion sometimes fades away when you are a fan. I would never suggest a fan work with their favorite artist or band. Because you will see or experience things that change your view of the band and initially excited you may be lost.

Ben Bledsoe
Singer-Songwriter/Composer/Actor
Ex-Natural
C.E.O. 44th Floor Records

How has the music business changed since you started your career? What's your opinion on the changes?

The record labels' worst fears have come to be, compared to when I first signed with BMG in 2000. My band's first album was made completely unreadable to computers for fear of the internet making it too easy to share music. Now digital downloads make up the majority of the income for musicians and labels worldwide. A lot of labels went under (including a few I was signed to), because they were too fearful of change and waited too long. Now, I feel like it's an even playing field for the first time in a hundred years. With talent and marketing savvy, anyone can make it. Like it or not. Labels no longer search for bands with potential to develop and nurture. Now artists have to go to a label with a finished product (Image, CD Master, proven fan-base, Logo, artwork, etc) for them to possibly release and market.

What advice would you give to young aspiring industry-types? What qualities did you find comforting in writers, label people, publicists, etc?

Probably the same thing you like in people that you work with. My favorite interviews were always the ones with people who actually cared about what I had to say. Whether it's because of their job or not, it makes an immense difference as an artist. It gets so boring answering the same mundane questions over and over and over a hundred times a day. When someone comes along and really wants to know your thoughts and about your life and experiences, your answers get much more interesting as well.

Where do you see the music industry going?

I hope to see it continue the way it is now. The old structure has collapsed, and the digital revolution is taking over. Sites like Pandora are making new music discoverable and purchasable to anyone interested in that genre. One of the biggest problems with the music industry is that there's no foundation for it. It's ultimately all chaos. If we can establish a database of credits for people based on who they represent/have represented, are producing/have produced, have recorded, mixed, mastered, etc., we can start a newer, more honest industry. Until now, everyone has been able to just kind of say what they want people to believe. There should be a place to show proof and research about who has worked with any released artist or band. Only then can the industry really start to fully bloom again.

Is being a fan more important than anything else?

I like the question. I don't know the answer though. As an artist, it's a 50/50 split for me. I never wrote the music "for" the fans. I always did the music for me. But there's nothing more amazing than knowing that what you've written has affected people in ways that you never imagined—changing the way they think. And I personally don't think you're ever on the other side of the coin anyway...You are constantly a fan of music no matter who you are. There are always people to learn from and inspire.

Gary Richards
Founder
Nitrus Records
HARD Festival

How has the music business changed since you started your career? What's your opinion on the changes?
Plain and simple people do not buy music anymore. Its really hurt the entire business side of things from top to bottom.

What advice would you give to young aspiring industry-types? What qualities did you find comforting in writers, label people, publicists, etc?
I would tell them to get the ball rolling on your own. Don't depend on someone else to get things moving for you in the biz.

Where do you see the music industry going?
I think the live side of the biz is where all the excitement is now.

Is being a fan more important than anything else?
Of course it all boils down to music and if your not a fan than why are you reading this?

INDEX

Dysfunction 21

E

Earth Crisis 67
Edge, Paul 94
Elektra 21
Eminem 91
Emotional Syphon Recordings 94, 105
Emperor 89
"Entertainment Weekly" 36
Epitaph 120

F

Facebook 28, 78
Fafara, Dez 92, 116
Family Values Tour 92, 125
Fear And The Nervous System 105
Fear Factory 93
Fehn, Chris 91
Filth, Dani 89, 115
Firm, The 125
"FMBQ" 9, 12-13, 15, 41-42
Follow The Leader 92
Ford, Joby 113
Fox Music 128
Fricke, David 14
Fu Manchu 122

G

Gargano, Paul 14, 81, 117
Gershon, Gina 12
Gitter, Mike 118
Glassjaw 89
God Forbid 26
Godhead 112
Gold, Benjie 130
"Good Morning America" 79
Google 22, 33, 68
Gossard, Stone 88, 90
Gray, Chad 92, 94
Greene, Ashley 80
"Guitar Hero" 110, 125
"Guitar World" 16, 42
GZA 107

H

"Hails & Horns" 16, 42
HARD Festival 132
Hard Rock Café 21
Hardwicke, Catherine 80
Hatebreed 40, 67, 89, 91

Hendrix, Jimi 78, 94
Hetfield, James 90
"High Fidelity" 120
Hit Parader 16, 38, 42, 53, 121
Hoffman, Phillip Seymour 119
Hot Topic 22, 38, 80
"Houses of the Holy" 120

I

I against I 120
Idol, Billy 111
Ill Nino 31
In Flames 88
Iron Maiden 112
Ishahn 89

J

Jackman, Hugh 80
Jackson , Samuel L. 37, 80
Jar of Flies 92
Jasta, Jamie 89
Johnson, Brian 21
Jordison, Joey 53, 91, 93
Juice 11, 15, 42

K

Katsis,Peter 125
Kebbel, Arielle 80
"Kerrang" 16, 42-43, 88, 91
Kinetic-9 107
Kittie 21
Korn 22, 27, 92-94, 124-125
Kristoff, Anne 21
Kwatinez, Jeff 125

L

"La Weekly" 123, 126
"Lax Magazine" 38, 80, 102
Leary, Denis 80
Led Zeppelin 110, 120
"Legally Blonde" 31
Levine/Schneider pr 127
Liotta, Ray 80
Linkin Park 28
"Little Miss Sunshine" 98
"Lollipop" 15
Ludacris 50

Amy Sciarretto is a 15-year veteran –although she looks all of 21-years-old— of the rock music scene and the most prolific female journalist in the metal scene who was recently profiled in the national trade mag *Radio & Records* where she was dubbed "The Queen Of Metal." An international rock journalist and bio writer who got her start when she was still in high school, she created columns (and wrote them for 5 years) when *Revolver* relaunched in 2001. She has written cover stories for international rock Bible *Kerrang!,* and through the years, her words have continuously appeared in the pages of *Alternative Press,* AOL Spinner, *Guitar World, Decibel, Hit Parader* (which she still co-edits), *CMJ New Music Report* (where she served as Loud Rock Editor for 8 years), *Spin.com, VH1.com, TeenPeople.com, CMJ New Music Monthly, FMQB, Outburn, Metal Maniacs, Chord, Sucker , , Amp, Hails & Horns, Ruin, music.com, Aquarian Weekly, Rockpile, ARTISTdirect, Ultimate Guitar, Rebel Ink, Urban Ink* and *LAX.* She was a weekend DJ on Sirius Satellite Radio's 24/7 metal channel Hard Attack for 2 years. All the while she has also served as Roadrunner's Director of Hard Rock Radio and Video Promotion for 6 years before being promoted to Director of Publicity/Media/Artist Relations in 2007. She has expanded into the mainstream women's journalism field, writing cosmetic and fashions stories for the popular site, *www.beautynewsnyc.com,* as well as writing about Fashion and Beauty trends as the Fashion/Beauty editor of the recently launched *LAX Magazine.* She has guested on countless radio platforms throughout the past decade and has been covering film and movies for a variety of the aforementioned publications for the past year. She lives outside of New York City in her native, beloved New Jersey and enjoys traveling, watching Philly sports teams and petting bulldog puppies on the mean streets of NYC.

Rick Florino has been working in the entertainment industry since 2004. At 19-years-old, upon graduating from Boston University Magna Cum Laude, he moved to Los Angeles from Massachusetts in order to pursue his dream of working in the biz. He started working at New Line Cinema and freelancing for magazines such as *Metal Edge, AMP* and *Lollipop.* Constantly writing, he cultivated a unique style that was clever, vivid and highly eloquent. That style would fuel his 2006 endeavor, *Ruin Magazine.* *Ruin* is a full-color glossy hard rock magazine carried in Hot Topic nationally that Rick founded. He sold the ads, wrote most of the stories and snapped a lot of the photos. Simultaneously, he worked as an editor for Citysearch.com, writing celebrity profiles and restaurant reviews. In 2007, Rick became an editor for ARTISTdirect.com, where he conducts interviews with A-list film and music talent for exclusive features and he reviews the hottest movies and CDs. He became the executive entertainment editor for *LAX Magazine* in 2008. For *LAX,* he specializes in cover stories and covering every facet of L.A. life—from celebrity to fitness. His words have appeared in publications including *Inked Magazine, BPM, Revolver, Hit Parader, Shockhound*.com and many more. He also writes bios for major record labels and publicity firms. He lives for movies and music, and his next endeavors are publishing a book of short fiction stories and selling one of his scripts. In addition, he loves to read, watch movies, box, take cooking classes, hang out at *The Grove* in Los Angeles, run, hike and play video games.

Printed in the United States
220834BV00002BA/2/P